THE SHUBERTS
OF BROADWAY

Jacob J., Sam, and Lee Shubert, the show business entrepreneurs who founded the largest theatre management and producing operation in America, the Shubert Organization, at the turn of the nineteenth century.

THE SHUBERTS
of
BROADWAY

A History Drawn from the Collections of the Shubert Archive

BROOKS McNAMARA

New York   Oxford
OXFORD UNIVERSITY PRESS
1990

ACKNOWLEDGMENTS: The author and publisher wish to acknowledge the use of photographs provided, with permission, by the following persons and institutions: ix, Beverly Sills; pages 10 (top), 13, 15, 18, 19, 24 (top), and 55, Museum of the City of New York; page 107, Mrs. Norman Elson; page 218, Stephen Vallillo. Material from letters written by George Bernard Shaw to Lee Shubert (pages 56, 57, and 58) is quoted with the permission of the Society of Authors on behalf of the George Bernard Shaw Estate. Material from *Playbill* used by permission. PLAY-BILL® is a registered trademark of Playbill Incorporated, NYC.

Oxford University Press

Oxford   New York   Toronto
Delhi   Bombay   Calcutta   Madras   Karachi
Petaling Jaya   Singapore   Hong Kong   Tokyo
Nairobi   Dar es Salaam   Cape Town
Melbourne   Auckland

and associated companies in
Berlin   Ibadan

Copyright © 1990 by Brooks McNamara

Published by Oxford University Press, Inc.,
200 Madison Avenue, New York, New York 10016

Oxford is a registered trademark of Oxford University Press

Library of Congress Cataloging-in-Publication Data
McNamara, Brooks.
The Shuberts of Broadway : a history drawn from the collections
of the Shubert Archive / Brooks McNamara.
p. cm.   Includes bibliographical references.
ISBN 0-19-506542-5
1. Shubert, Lee, 1875?-1953.   2. Shubert, Sam S., 1877?-1905.
3. Shubert, Jacob J., 1879?-1963.   4. Theater—New York (N.Y.)-History
—20th century.   5. Theater—United States—History—20th century.
6. Theatrical producers and directors—United States—Biography.
7. Theatrical paraphernalia—United States.
8. Shubert family.   I. Shubert Archive.   II. Title.
PN2285.M335   1990
792'.0232'09227471—dc20   90-31422

2 4 6 8 9 7 5 3 1
Printed in the United States of America
on acid-free paper

To Nan, Jane, and Whitney

FOREWORD
Beverly Sills

In December of 1944, when I was fifteen years old, my singing teacher Estelle Liebling arranged an audition for me. I was to sing excerpts from *The Pirates of Penzance* and *The Merry Widow* for her old friend J. J. Shubert. Mr. J. J. was planning two national touring companies, one of which would perform Gilbert and Sullivan operas, and the other *The Merry Widow* and *Rosemarie*.

My mother and I arrived by subway from Brooklyn. Mr. J. J. took one look at my mother and told her she was beautiful enough to be in the movies. He then turned his attention to me. "Do you ever wear high-heeled shoes?" he asked me.

"No she doesn't. She's only fifteen," my mother answered.

"Do you ever wear make-up?" he asked me.

"No she doesn't. She's only fifteen," my mother answered.

"Do you ever wear your hair in an upsweep?" he asked me.

"No she doesn't. She's only fifteen," my mother answered.

He shook his head rather resignedly. "Okay," he said, "sing for me." I did—and he applauded when I finished "Vilea."

I did those two tours. But not without some hard negotiating between him and my mother. Since she could not accompany me on the tour, a proper chaperone had to be mutually agreed upon. You see, my father thought that women who went on the stage were "hussies." They wore low-cut dresses, too much make-up and dyed their hair. But my mother's primary purpose in life was to give her children a chance to dream and then to help make those dreams come

Beverly Sills on tour for the Shuberts: programs for Play, Gypsy Play *(1946; a retreaded version of Lee and J.J.'s success from the twenties,* Countess Maritza*) and* The Merry Widow *(1947); and a cast photograph of Sills (center) in the title role from* The Merry Widow.

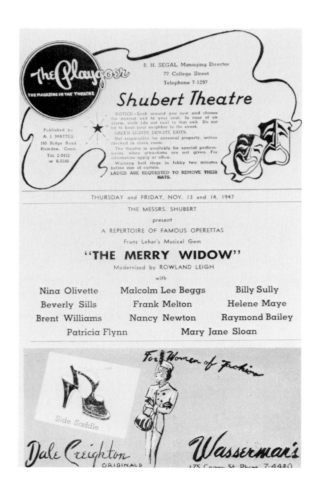

true. I dreamed of being an opera star, and therefore I would be one. End of argument. So Mr. J. J. and my mom found a terrific girl. She would be my companion, chaperone, hairdresser, and make-up person. She was fabulous. She had only two weaknesses: gin and airline pilots.

On the tour I was billed as "The Youngest Prima Donna in Captivity." J. J. bought me my first high-heeled shoes, my first pair of false eyelashes, and decided I would look better as a redhead. The first time my father saw me in *The Merry Widow,* he came backstage after the performance and, with a big twinkle in his eye, said, "You see? A low-cut dress, too much make-up and a different color hair—I told you!—but you sang like an angel." I called Mr. J. J. to tell him what my Dad had said and he told me, "You'll never have a better or more important review in your life." He was right.

I loved Mr. J. J. He sent me jigsaw puzzles and crossword puzzles on tour. I suspect I'm not the only one whose life was dramatically influenced by him. And I know that the history of the theatre in our country would have a totally different story to tell if the Shubert name was not involved. That's why I'm so pleased to be a part of *The Shuberts of Broadway*. It creates a wonderful and telling portrait of the Shuberts and their world. All of us owe an enormous debt to people who influence our culture, who inspire us to dream by showing us worlds we never knew existed, and who stir up a little excitement and controversy while they're at it. The Shuberts did all those things.

April 18, 1990

PREFACE

Very little has been written in recent years about the Shubert brothers. A few articles touch on them, usually as background for a discussion of the current activities of the Shubert Organization, the company they founded in New York City ninety years ago. By far the most interesting treatment of the Shuberts is an early three-part *New Yorker* profile, "The Boys from Syracuse," by A. J. Liebling, published in 1939. Liebling's account, based on interviews with Lee and J.J., catches the essence of their complex personalities as no other work does.

The only book about the Shuberts was published in 1968 by the late Jerry Stagg, a screenwriter and television producer. Stagg's *The Brothers Shubert* is, in many ways, still a useful work, and I have found it essential in trying to understand the Shuberts' far-flung business affairs. But, as its author would certainly have admitted, he did not like the Shuberts. His book concentrates on the most sanguinary aspects of their business dealings and he pays little attention to their roles as play producers and theatre builders.

In writing *The Shuberts of Broadway* I have tried to fill some of the gaps left by Stagg's account. Because company records are available for the first time in the newly created Shubert Archive, I have emphasized what they tell us about Sam, Lee, and J.J. Shubert. My focus has been on discussing plays and theatres, and on developing a brief outline of the Shubert brothers' place in the history of Broadway and in the whole of American show business. Much more remains to be done, but I hope that this first work based on the Shubert Archive will lead researchers to an extraordinary new resource in the history of American entertainment.

Especially useful documents from the Archive have included letters written by family members and letters and reports addressed to them. Also helpful were the Archive's extensive clipping files on the family, as well as the company's early press-office files relating to shows produced by the three Shubert brothers. Wherever possible, I have identified these materials briefly when I first mention them in the text. Unless otherwise noted, quotations from Lee and John Shubert are taken from autobiographical fragments in the Archive. I frequently quote from published books and articles, and I have included a selected bibliography which should be useful to researchers. Also useful to anyone interested in the Shuberts and the holdings of the Shubert Archive is "The Passing Show," a newsletter published semiannually by the Archive since 1977.

A limited number of illustrations, especially for the earliest years, come from sources other than the Shubert Archive, in particular the remarkable Theatre Collection of the Museum of the City of New York. When the source of a picture is not the Shubert Archive, I have noted its origin in the Acknowledgments. I am grateful to Robert Taylor, former Curator of the Theatre Collection at the Museum of the City of New York, and to Faith Coleman, a former MCNY staff member, for their assistance in locating important pictorial material. My thanks are also due to Dorothy Swerdlove and her staff at the Billy Rose Theatre Collection at the New York Public Library at Lincoln Center for additional items. Kevin Lewis, formerly on the staff of the Shubert Archive, located many of the pictures in this book. His help was invaluable.

I will always be grateful for the contributions of present and former staff members of the Archive, especially Brigitte Kueppers, Maryann Chach, Reagan Fletcher, Mark Swartz, and to my research assistants Andrea Stulman Dennett and Elizabeth Hess. Errors should be laid at my door, and not at theirs.

Finally, I wish to thank the John Simon Guggenheim Foundation, whose Fellowship helped to make this work possible, and the Tisch School of the Arts at New York University, which provided me with release time from my other duties to develop the Shubert Archive, and my editors, Sheldon Meyer, Karen Wolny, and Leona Capeless. The vision and enthusiasm of four individuals made this book—and indeed the whole Shubert archive project—a reality. My sincerest thanks to Gerald Schoenfeld, Chairman of the Shubert Organization; Bernard B. Jacobs, President; Lynn Seidler, Director of the Shubert Foundation; and Robert Wankel, Vice-President of the Shubert Organization. Truly, none of this work could have happened without them.

New York City   Brooks McNamara
April 1990

CONTENTS

INTRODUCTION
Searching for the Shuberts

*A word to anyone looking for the original
script of "The Whistling Oyster": It's been
found. The sheet music to "The Girl and the
Kaiser" turned up, too. And, yes, the photograph of Maestro Buddy Swann, the child
conductor of the "Hellzapoppin'" pit band,
has been unearthed.*

SAMUEL G. FREEDMAN,
The New York Times,
September 25, 1985

In New York City, not far from where I live, is a shop called Urban
Archaeology, which specializes in such remnants of the city's architectural past as iron work, stained glass, and the gargoyles from
Victorian brownstones. The odd name always strikes a special chord
with me because, for the last thirteen years, I have been involved in an
urban archaeology project of my own—one of a very different sort,
but an exercise in urban archaeology all the same. It centers on the
Broadway theatre, and it has involved locating, rescuing, and organ-
izing millions of documents connected with the history of Broadway.
   One day in the spring of 1976, I was asked by the Shubert Foundation to look over what was modestly referred to as "some papers"
related to the three Shubert brothers, Sam, Lee, and Jacob J. (usually
known as J.J.). I assumed at the time that I had several weeks of work
ahead of me. The next day, however, I was shown a three-story
storage area in the wings of the Shubert Theatre filled to the rafters
with crates and boxes and filing cabinets. It was only the beginning.
Over the next week, I was taken to rooms in other theatres that were

packed with the memorabilia of the difficult and controversial men who controlled much of American show business during the first half of the twentieth century. I soon discovered that lofts, attics, and basements all over the Broadway area were still overflowing with papers, plans, and drawings, more than a decade after the death of J.J., the last survivor of the three brothers. There were two rooms filled with orchestra parts in the Imperial Theatre, and a penthouse on top of the Longacre Theatre was crammed with music, costume designs, play scripts—even a trunk full of Chinese robes purchased by J.J. Shubert on some long-forgotten trip to the Orient.

But this was the tip of the iceberg. It quickly became obvious that there were other caches of scripts and letters and architectural plans in most of the out-of-town theatres as well—more than twenty buildings in all. Although Sam died in 1905, shortly after the founding of the Shuberts' New York operation, his brothers lived on for many years, and both were compulsive savers of records connected with their activities. Many things were discarded after the deaths of Lee

A room in the wings of the Shubert Theatre, New York City, in which early company business correspondence was stored for many years; and Lee Shubert's dining room in his penthouse on top of the same theatre. When the Shubert Archive was started in 1976, the old dining room had long been used for the storage of scripts, music, and art objects belonging to the Shubert brothers. Much of the business material found in the wings of the Shubert Theatre dates back to the first two decades of the twentieth century and documents the earliest years of the brothers' activities in New York and on the road. Much more material about the company's history was located in other Shubert theatres on Broadway and across the country.

and J.J., but the amount of material that had survived into the mid-seventies was phenomenal. A rough survey made about the time I first examined the records suggested that there were, in one space or another, the equivalent of perhaps 1500 file drawers of material. Since then, new discoveries have resulted in our filling a five-story building with the Shubert papers—altogether some four million items.

After those first few days, it was clear that the job was a far bigger one than anyone had thought, and I was more than a little hesitant to agree that I could put this vast hoard in order. I was a full-time faculty member at New York University, and I could not imagine how I would manage to organize the apparently endless Shubert papers as well. The answer came when an old friend, Brigitte Kueppers, a theatre librarian at the New York Public Library, agreed to join me on the project, handling all of the actual day-by-day organization. New York University came to my rescue by giving me time off from teaching, and the Shubert Foundation arranged to hire a number of graduate students from my department as assistants. By the fall of 1976, we were fairly launched.

The problem now was to gain control over this mountain range of material. There might be a room filled with papers at one theatre, a closetful at another, two or three filing cabinets at a third. We began touring every theatre, marking down those things that most needed to be brought to some central location. In the meantime, we took up temporary quarters in a penthouse on top of the Longacre Theatre, in which a very large amount of material had already been stored over the years. The space would do for the moment, but it was clear that it would house only a fraction of the total collection, and I began to ask everyone I came across for leads about a better location for the Archive.

In our hunt for a more workable space, we were shown two floors at the top of the Shubert Organization's Lyceum Theatre on Forty-fifth Street, a landmark building and the oldest operating Broadway house, first opened in 1903. We soon moved into a former rehearsal hall on the top floor. A few months later the floor below became vacant and we acquired what had been the penthouse apartment of the theatre's builder, producer Daniel Frohman. In recent years the space had been cut up into a series of small offices; but it was apparent at once that, underneath the changes, the apartment was basically intact and little altered since Frohman's day.

Frohman's personal suite (with its famous hatch in the dining-room wall through which he watched the show each night) became our main offices, and his top-floor rehearsal hall was turned into a workroom and storage area. But once again we were almost immediately out of space. We turned next to Frohman's old scene-painters' and carpenters' lofts in the rear of the building and eventually remodeled them into library stacks.

It was in one of Frohman's old lofts that we housed the flood of orchestra parts that came to us from the Century Library, the contents of which had somehow miraculously survived almost intact. The Century Library was a play-leasing operation, handling virtually all of the dramatic works controlled by the Shuberts, including many of their musicals. Through a card catalogue inherited by the Archive it was still possible to locate every play manuscript, every orchestra part, every song, and every revue sketch ever leased by the Century Library—a collection that once filled a published catalogue of more than 150 pages.

An entire floor of the Lyceum is now filled with the Century Library music, including material from such Shubert classics as *The Student Prince, Rose Marie, Blossom Time,* and various editions of *Artists and Models, Gay Paree,* and the later *Ziegfeld Follies,* which were co-produced by the Shuberts and Billie Burke after Ziegfeld's death in 1932. On hand, too, are the scores for no less than seventeen editions of J.J. Shubert's famous Winter Garden revue *The Passing Show,* an annual summer event after 1912. We have also located programs, press clippings, script material, and scenic and costume designs for several hundred other shows.

Discoveries continue to be made. About 2000 revue sketches, for example, surfaced a few years ago in a pair of filing cabinets that were almost buried under a pile of used furniture; and costume designs and posters often appear in packages of orchestra parts or tucked in among the pages of letters from agents or managers. More than 8000 sheets of architectural plans have been located, making up what must be the best single resource on American theatre architecture. Some of the plans date back to the early years of the century and offer silent

Producer Daniel Frohman's Lyceum Theatre in New York as it appeared a few years after its opening in 1903 (the Lyceum is now a Shubert theatre and the home of the Shubert Archive); a corner of Frohman's penthouse apartment on top of the Lyceum in the early years; the same corner today (the penthouse now serves as the reading room for the Shubert Archive; shown in the photograph are the first archivist, Brigitte Kueppers, the author, and Lynn Seidler, Executive Director of the Shubert Foundation).

testimony to the vast network of theatres once assembled by the Shuberts. "In their heyday, 1927," says Gerald Schoenfeld, chairman of the Shubert Organization, "the brothers owned or operated 104 theatres, and they must have booked a thousand." Blueprints for many of these theatres have survived and have found their way into the Archive. Among the most interesting are the many plans drawn by the Shubert "house architect," Herbert J. Krapp, the designer of such famous Broadway theatres as the Majestic, the Broadhurst, and the Imperial.

Another collection provides a glimpse of the Shuberts in a different medium. The Archive contains about seventy radio transcriptions from the 1940s and 50s, chiefly from *The Chicago Theatre of the Air*, which was broadcast on WGN in Chicago, and *The Railroad Hour*, broadcast from Los Angeles. For these once-famous radio shows, such musicals as *Countess Maritza, My Maryland, The Fire Fly*, and *Frederika* were condensed to a one-hour format. There are no less than eight radio versions of the immensely popular *Student Prince*.

But radio was not the brothers' only venture outside the theatre. Although few people are aware of it today, the Shuberts were very much involved in the motion picture business during the teens, as producers, exhibitors, and distributors. They owned their own studio in Fort Lee, New Jersey, and one of their motion picture staff members once blithely prophesied that the Shuberts' World Film Corporation, together with Paramount, could come to dominate American film production. The rest is history—in its last years, before the studio was destroyed by fire, it served as a warehouse for scenery and for the art and antiques brought back by J.J. from his frequent European tours. Shubert Vaudeville—two short-lived forays outside the legitimate theatre—is also enshrined in the Archive papers, along with the World War II entertainment efforts of Lee and J.J., and especially J.J.'s son John, who created shows for the armed forces.

Over the years, we have come across such treasures as a contract between the Shuberts and Mark Twain for a dramatization of *Huckleberry Finn*, a file of correspondence with George Bernard Shaw about his schemes for an American production of one of his plays, and the papers of a road manager who impounded the trunk of an A.W.O.L. actress. The files—and the stories they contain—sometimes seem to have no end. Almost from the first it was apparent that the Archive would provide the raw material for dozens of exhibitions, articles, and books, and in 1978, I organized an exhibit of some 300 items at the Shubert Theatre in Los Angeles with museum designer Don Vlack. A second exhibit with Vlack followed ten years later. These exhibits led ultimately to this book, which I hope will illustrate the range of the Shubert brothers' involvement in American show business and serve as a sample of the collection we have assembled at the Shubert Archive.

Perhaps a word needs to be said about the theatres and the plays discussed in *The Shuberts of Broadway*. The Archive contains material on several hundred theatres built, purchased, or leased by the Shuberts over half a century, as well as information on more than 500 plays produced by them. I have seen no compelling reason to try to consider all of the theatres or all of the plays in this book. In discussing theatres, I have focused on representative Shubert houses, and especially on the great Broadway houses that have survived down to the present day.

As for the plays, the Shubert brothers were first and foremost producers of light "commercial" comedies, mysteries, musicals, revues, and operettas. All of them are of some interest as period documents, but most have not worn well down through the years and are of little concern to the general reader of today. Even Lee—who presented a certain number of classics and "serious" dramas—made no bones about the Shuberts' pragmatic approach to selecting plays for production. In 1921 he outlined that approach to an interviewer for *American Magazine.*

"We have learned a few things, at least," Lee said. "We know that people like youth and beauty. We know that they will go down in their pockets and pay gladly, if you will give them something that will make them laugh. They like to see a play that holds their attention, keeps it from straying off to their worries and troubles. Probably that is the reason they are so keen about something new. People want a play to have plenty of action. A few persons will go to a 'talky' play and be interested, if the talk is clever and brilliant. But those persons form a very small group."

Lee and J.J. were, in short, producers of popular entertainments, involved in show business rather than art. In many ways they fit more comfortably with the early motion picture moguls—whom they undoubtedly influenced—than with such "artistic" or socially committed producers as the Provincetown Players, the Theatre Guild, or the Mercury Theatre. In fact, their producing policies were precisely what such groups were reacting against from the teens onward. New York, Lee told the *American Magazine*, is the "theatrical manufacturing city of the country." For half a century, Lee and J.J. were America's principal *manufacturers* of theatrical productions. Their careers need to be understood in that light if they are to be understood at all.

THE SHUBERTS
OF BROADWAY

I
THE EARLY YEARS

We were boys, young and energetic, and we took a great many chances because we had very little.

J.J. SHUBERT
Letter to John Shubert, 1952

In 1948 a reporter named Inez Robb wrote a wire-service story in which she noted that "there is no arguing the fact that the Shuberts dominate and govern Broadway, through ownership of half the city's theatres. But they are aloof from it. They are in it, but not of it." The Shuberts, she said, talk to "nobody, no time, no place—unless it is strictly business."

It was a telling point; over the years the Shubert brothers had become famous for their reluctance to reveal anything of substance about their plans, their private lives, or their backgrounds. Indeed, Lee and J.J. treated their personal histories like press releases, reshaping them as needed, casually editing out anything that did not seem to serve their purposes at the moment. J.J. variously listed the year of his birth as 1876, 1877, 1879, and 1880. He was born in Syracuse, New York, or in East Prussia or in Poland. He married his first wife in New York City or in France. Lee was Sam Shubert's older brother—or his younger brother. The occasion for Robb's article was Lee's divorce from a woman to whom no one knew he had been married. The family name was Szemanski, or it was Shubert or Schubert or Shubard.

Catherine ("Carrie") Shubert; David Shubert; and the family home in Syracuse. The man in front of the house is a former tenant. According to John Shubert, his grandparents were desperately poor during their Syracuse days: "By the time of Dora's birth, the two eldest boys, Sam and Lee, were pitifully trying to help the family out with scraps of wood and pieces of coal they hunted for in the nearby freight yard. Tragically, their efforts were still not enough to ensure the Shuberts' retaining even a modest larder . . . [their sister] Lisa, a thin, consumptive child from birth, died of malnutrition."

As a result, there are few clear-cut answers about the family's early history, although old records in the Shubert Archive suggest that the family name was originally Shubert, or some variation of it, and that the Shuberts were poor Jews from the East Prussian town of Neustadt, about forty miles from Danzig. Lee (probably Levi) was apparently born in 1875, Sam in 1877, and Jacob J. in 1879. All of them seem to have been born in or around Neustadt, as were their sisters Fanny, Sarah, and Lisa. Lisa died—probably in Syracuse, New York—shortly after the birth of a fourth daughter, Dora.

Their father, David, was apparently living in Syracuse as early as 1882, although the rest of the family probably did not follow him there until several years later. Census reports suggest that all the Shuberts were living in the shabby Seventh Ward of Syracuse by 1892. There is a family story that David Shubert had been a tea smuggler in Europe and that he got the money to emigrate by informing on another smuggler, his father-in-law. In any case, he was a less than exemplary character—an unsuccessful peddler, an alcoholic, and a miserable provider. His sons seem to have disliked David Shubert intensely, and they pensioned him off many years before his death in 1913.

Their mother Catherine (usually called Carrie) appears to have been the exact opposite of her husband—industrious, hard driving, and extremely ambitious for her sons. In a desperate attempt to make ends meet, she ran a kind of boarding house for peddlers in her home. All three of the boys were as attached to their mother as they were contemptuous of their father, and after their first success in New York they would arrange for her to live in style until her death, in 1914.

The three boys grew up on the streets. By the time Lee was ten years old he was shining shoes and selling newspapers in front of the Wieting Theatre in downtown Syracuse. Before long he was joined by Sam. In a piece of serendipity that was to have far-reaching consequences, Sam was chosen to appear as a walk-on in a touring production of producer David Belasco's *May Blossom*. The theatre clearly looked more appealing than any of Sam's other options, and he moved on to become a program boy at the nearby Bastable Theatre, and later a ticket seller at the Syracuse Grand Opera House. It was obvious to everyone that Sam was both unusually bright and a fantastically hard worker. In an autobiographical fragment, Lee recalled his brother as an unusual child, "with zeal and self-assurance that inspired confidence and made friends." By the early nineties, when Sam was no more than seventeen, he had become head of the box office at the Wieting.

The vast majority of the shows for which Sam sold tickets were popular farces, melodramas, and musical extravaganzas. Although interest in serious realistic plays was beginning to develop, the popular playwright dominated the American theatre during the last quarter of the nineteenth century. At the forefront was a writer named Charles Hoyt, whom Sam met at the Wieting. The meeting turned out to be a fortuitous one. Even in a time when there were fortunes to be made as a popular playwright, Hoyt was something of a phenomenon. A millionaire before he was thirty, he turned out more than a play a year from the early eighties to his death at the end of the century. With one or two exceptions, his plays were always highly successful and extremely profitable. One of the best was *A Texas Steer,* a slapstick comedy about Washington politics written in 1890. It was this play that launched the Shuberts as theatrical producers in 1894. Because Hoyt was impressed with Sam's ability, he sold him the rights to produce his Broadway success on tour. Sam cleared $10,000, a considerable sum for the time.

With *A Texas Steer* the family's fortunes turned a critical corner. The next spring Sam added Hoyt's *A Contented Woman* and *A Stranger in New York* to his tour and began to think about acquiring theatres. As Lee described it, "his restless imagination quickly envisioned a chain of playhouses and productions of his own, a dream that his native shrewdness and tireless energy were to translate into reality when still but a boy." Sam leased the Bastable in Syracuse, then swiftly took over the Majestic in Utica, the Rand Opera House in Troy, and theatres in Albany and Syracuse. A group of Shubert backers now financed a new theatre in Rochester, the Baker, which was managed by the brothers. Robert Grau, in *Forty Years Observation of Music and the Drama,* published in 1909, characterized the backers' faith in Sam—perhaps with a slight edge. "Sam Shubert," he wrote, "was an electric battery when set in motion, a veritable bundle of nerves, and his marvelous energy attracted the attention of several

Charles Hoyt. Lee recalled that Hoyt was at first somewhat surprised and "a trifle skeptical" when the very young Sam Shubert approached him with the idea of forming a road company of his play A Texas Steer. But "Sam had little difficulty in raising the money," Lee wrote, "after which he went to New York, bought the rights to the play and production, engaged a company and took A Texas Steer on tour, the first attraction to be presented under Shubert management, and from the start a money maker for him and his backers."

Program, 1898, from the Bastable Theatre, Syracuse, N.Y., managed by the young Sam Shubert. Another Syracuse house, controlled by the powerful Theatrical Syndicate, automatically received all of the first-class productions that came to town. As Lee told it, the Shubert brothers "took into the Bastable whatever independent attractions we could find, but they were not numerous enough or good enough to make the policy profitable, so we installed a permanent stock company which was operated with considerable success." It was the first of many brushes between the Shuberts and the Syndicate.

gentlemen in the mercantile line who were glad of the opportunity to invest their capital with so competent and pushing a manipulator."

J.J. was put in charge of the Baker. The Shuberts installed a successful stock company there and hired a young resident playwright and director named Owen Davis, who would later achieve fame of a sort as the author of more than a hundred spectacular melodramas, among them *Her One False Step* and *Nellie, the Beautiful Cloak Model*. Davis's extraordinary ability to create a reasonably stage-worthy script at short notice endeared him to the Shuberts, who, from the first, kept a close eye on both expenses and on popular taste. As Grau phrased it, "the three brothers began to operate with the precision which was destined to place them, in a few years, in the very front rank" of managers.

As the nineteenth century came to an end, the Shubert brothers were managing several stock companies and five upstate theatres, and they were about to take the next logical step—a Shubert theatre on Broadway. In 1900, Sam and Lee signed a lease on the Herald Square Theatre at the northwest corner of Broadway and Thirty-fifth Street. The area from which the theatre took its name was a kind of way-station between the great nineteenth-century theatrical center at Union Square, some twenty blocks to the south, and the new theatre district, half a dozen blocks to the north near Times Square. In 1900 a healthy sprinkling of theatres, including the Metropolitan Opera House and Oscar Hammerstein's gigantic Olympia, already dotted the landscape above Herald Square. The Square itself was in the process of losing its theatrical identity and was soon to become a major shopping center and the home of Macy's and Gimbel's department stores. But at the turn of the century the Herald Square Theatre, built in 1883, was still in operation.

In 1894, Charles Evans, the manager of the theatre, had begun to feature a stock company led by Broadway star Richard Mansfield. Six years later the house generally booked miscellaneous attractions, most of them of no particular consequence. But the lease was cheap, and with the financial backing of a friendly Syracuse haberdasher, Sam and Lee became Broadway theatre managers. J.J. remained in charge of the upstate theatre chain. Within a short time, Sam and Lee were to take over the leases on two other minor Broadway houses,

Sam, Lee, and Jacob J. Shubert as young men. In his 1912 autobiography, Fifty Years in Theatrical Management, *M. B. Leavitt characterized the Shubert brothers as "unique among the theatrical personalities of New York." He recalled Sam as "an indefatigable worker," whose "endurance, courage and willingness were wonderful," and who "always found time to show his good will toward his fellow-men." Lee, Leavitt said, "is the dreamer and schemer," and J.J., "the ultra practical man of the combination, and the 'shock absorber.' He takes the jolts and rides over them without a quiver. He has a habit of 'getting down to cases' immediately and staying there."*

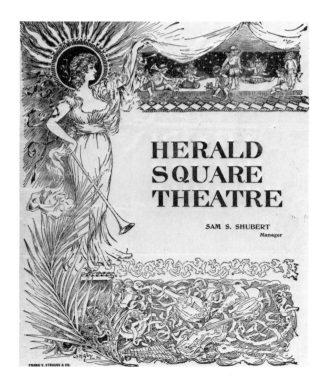

HERALD SQUARE THEATRE

SAM S. SHUBERT
Manager

FRANK V. STRAUSS & CO.

The Herald Square Theatre, the first Shubert house in New York City: a program cover from the period of Sam's management; and a photograph showing the Herald Square as it appeared about 1895, a few years before it was leased by the Shuberts. By 1912, Lee and J.J. had given up the house, presumably because by then it was too far south of the center of theatrical activity. The Herald Square became a movie theatre for several years before it was razed and a commercial building constructed on the site.

which had more or less been left behind as the theatre district moved north—the old Madison Square Theatre, a dozen blocks below Herald Square, at Broadway and Twenty-fourth Street, and near by, a former burlesque and minstrel house called the San Francisco Music Hall, which Sam and Lee renamed the Princess.

The Shuberts' lease on the Herald Square contained a clause which required them to honor all of the previous booking arrangements negotiated for the house, and it was obvious that they would have to produce their own shows around the theatre's prior commitments. Somehow, between those commitments, the novice producers managed to recall Mansfield to the Herald Square for a highly profitable engagement. Their first star was every bit as complex and difficult as any of the Shuberts. But Mansfield at the turn of the century was at the peak of his career as a romantic actor, and he was clearly a fantastic catch for the young managers, who seem to have struck a chord with him because of their business acumen and their thirst for success.

Lee would later see their triumph with Mansfield as a result of Sam's charismatic personality: "his direct convincing manner . . . inspired confidence that he knew his business and was able to carry out successfully anything that he undertook. A dozen older, established managers in New York would have jumped at the opportunity to secure Richard Mansfield for their theatres, and here was a boy not yet twenty years of age who had won this difficult, exacting, and opinionated star over at the first contact." Sam also managed to convince Mansfield to step into a failing Shubert play, *Old Heidelberg*. The result was a resounding success, and the play would later become the basis for one of the brothers' greatest musical hits, *The Student Prince*. The association continued for several years, and in 1903 the Shuberts would lease the new Lyric Theatre on Forty-second Street to house a yearly engagement of the Mansfield company, as well as the American School of Opera, a training organization headed by Reginald De Koven, composer of the sensationally successful 1891 comic opera *Robin Hood*.

In addition to capturing Mansfield for the Herald Square, the Shuberts had also managed to sign an agreement with the Theatrical Syndicate, turning the theatre into a Syndicate-affiliated house. The

Shubert mythology has it that, from the very start of their Broadway careers, the brothers were locked in mortal combat with Abraham Erlanger and the other members of the Syndicate. And yet, at the beginning, they were anything but opposed to it. In fact, they needed its patronage to survive in New York and on the road, since it was with the Syndicate that real theatrical power resided in 1900.

The Shubert brothers had begun their careers in a kind of theatre that was rapidly disappearing from the American scene. In the years just after the Civil War the resident stock company reached its height. Local companies, with a more or less permanent core of actors and a repertory of standard plays, represented the traditional approach to theatre organization. But as early as the middle of the century, stars had begun to take along their own cadre of supporting actors when they appeared with local stock companies. It was only a short step to the so-called "combination" company of the late 1870s, in which a star toured with a complete production, including cast, costumes, scenery, and properties.

Many managers—the Shuberts among them—continued to operate traditional stock companies, often employing them to present shows between star engagements and to tour while a star's company occupied their own theatre. But the growth of the railroads, which made it possible to move large shows with relative ease, was ultimately to destroy the resident repertory company. By the late nineties, the traveling road show, touring a long-run hit from New York, had become the typical fare around the country, and the time was right for the theatrical entrepreneur. As a result, in 1896, a group of six men

The Lyric Theatre (at left) early in the century. The Lyric, which opened in October of 1903, was a large, lavishly decorated house located on Forty-second Street near Seventh Avenue, the emerging center of Broadway show business. Lee called the theatre "the handsomest in New York at the time." Its opening, he wrote, was a triumph for Sam, "whose judgment and zeal had made the occasion possible." The Shuberts had their offices in the Lyric for some years, and Lee and J.J. would continue to produce there as late as 1917; during the thirties the theatre became a motion picture house, which it remains today.

had worked out a plan which would in effect give them financial control over the American theatre. The six—Marc Klaw, Abraham Erlanger, Charles Frohman, Al Hayman, Sam Nixon, and J. Fred Zimmerman—already dominated theatre in most major cities. Taking a leaf from the book of the other industrialists of the period, they merged their interests as a trust. Gradually, using whatever form of persuasion seemed necessary, they came to own, lease, or control the booking of more than 700 theatres across the country—and virtually to exclude competition.

The Syndicate offered some distinct benefits to producers and theatre owners. At the time, the booking of shows into theatres on the road was a relatively hit-or-miss business. Local managers booked their own shows, coming to New York each year to negotiate with dozens of different producers for the best dates and attractions. The Syndicate instigated a central clearinghouse which ensured a reasonably efficient flow of shows into participating theatres. The problem lay in the fact that the partners put great pressure on theatres to become Syndicate houses—and on producers and managers to deal exclusively with member theatres, forcing them to pay exorbitant booking charges for the privilege. Those who did not choose to cooperate had little option but to use poor or makeshift theatres or to be frozen out altogether.

"The scheme in its main workings was a simple one," a journalist named Colgate Baker wrote later in the Shuberts' *New York Review.* "A play, no matter how successful in New York, if it is to make any money on the road, must have its tour booked so that a performance can be given every evening at a town where the receipts will pay the railroad fares and leave something over." Baker went on to point out that it is of little use to play in "New York, in Boston, Washington, Chicago, St. Louis, Denver, and San Francisco, if you cannot play in the smaller towns between to pay your hauling charges. The Syndicate, either by leasehold or by promises to the local theatre managers to give them an uninterrupted season of attractions, rapidly controlled the approaches to the big cities, even when independent theatres were left in the cities themselves, and thus it controlled the theatrical situation in America."

At the outset, then, it was very much in the Shuberts' interest, as the smallest of small theatrical fry, to establish a workable connection with the Syndicate if they were to survive and flourish as producers and managers. And, in fact, the Shuberts were already doing very well indeed. In 1900 the brothers had picked up the touring rights to a musical called *The Belle of New York* at a bargain price. The show, a kind of early precursor of *Guys and Dolls,* revolved around the adventures of a Salvation Army lass named Violet Gray, who reforms a young spendthrift man about town, Harry Brown. Edna May, the daughter of a Syracuse postman and a friend of the Shuberts since childhood, played the title character. Although it had a modest Broadway run, *The Belle of New York* was to endure remarkably well; it toured profitably, became the first American musical comedy to run for more than a year in London's West End, and would be revived by the Shuberts as late as 1921 at the Winter Garden in a version called *The Whirl of New York.*

A second piece of serendipity was Augustus Thomas's *Arizona.* The play was an inherited one, already booked into the Herald

Harry Davenport and Edna May in the 1897 production of The Belle of New York, *which was toured with great success by the Shuberts. Davenport was the son of the well-known Shakespearean actor E. L. Davenport. May, a longtime friend of the Shuberts, became an instant star as a result of the show's popularity. Her character, Violet Gray, is described in a song from the show as "a great little girl, in a queer little gown, / Who's the pride of the Salvation Army, / And when she appears in this part of town, / Why she makes the whole neighborhood barmy."*

Square when the Shuberts took it over. Thomas was a prominent playwright of the day, and *Arizona,* although it seems like little more than a conventional Western melodrama today, was hailed by critics as an important realistic play. It ran for some eighteen weeks during the 1900–1901 season and, ironically, added a certain cachet to the Shuberts' reputation as producers.

But Sam and Lee still had not had a chance to produce in New York totally on their own. In May of 1901, however, they managed to squeeze one of their own productions into the Herald Square, an undistinguished English play called *The Brixton Burglary,* which featured the young Lionel Barrymore in a small role and managed a six-week run. The Shuberts were now launched as Broadway producers in their own right, and by the next year they had an authentic hit, an English musical called *A Chinese Honeymoon,* which opened in June of 1902 at their newly acquired Casino Theatre.

A Chinese Honeymoon, with a book by George Dance and music by Howard Talbot, had been a spectacular success in London, where it ran for more than 1000 performances. The plot, such as it is, involves one Simon Pineapple and his bride, who spend their wedding trip to China in a series of comic adventures. Pineapple is continually caught flirting with a quartet of bridesmaids, and Mrs. Pineapple flirts with a bill poster who turns out to be the Emperor incognito. Mr. Pineapple's nephew, Tom, along for the honeymoon, is pursued by an amorous waitress named Fi Fi. In the guise of a doctor, Tom in turn pursues the Emperor's niece Soo Soo. *A Chinese Honeymoon* turned out to be the hit of the season and managed almost a year's run at the Casino, as well as a substantial road tour.

The lease on the Casino, the Shuberts' second major New York theatre, had only been acquired after a farce-comedy court battle with rival leasees, the Sire brothers. For their trouble, the Shuberts got an uninhibited piece of high-Victorian architecture, which had opened in 1882 on the southeast corner of Broadway and Thirty-ninth Street. The impresario Rudolph Aronson had run a resident light opera company in the building for a number of years. Eventually, however, the Casino became a booking house, and by 1900 it had gained more than passing fame as the home of the hit English musical *Florodora,*

An advertising card for A Chinese Honeymoon. *The show featured Thomas Q. Seabrook, a specialist in Irish comedy roles. Like many other musicals of its day, it contained an interpolated comedy song that was designed to stop the show and was totally unrelated to the plot. "Mr. Dooley," sung by Seabrook in the role of Mr. Pineapple, was a tribute to journalist Finley Peter Dunne's Irish bartender-philosopher, whose syndicated reflections on life and politics were all the rage. "Mr. Dooley, Mr. Dooley," the chorus runs, "To Edison he taught a thing or two, / And young Marconi, eats macaroni, / Along with Mr. Dooley-ooley-oo."*

produced by Shubert ally George Lederer—a show which J.J. was to revive with great success in 1920.

At the Shuberts' Herald Square in September of 1902 was another prestigious English show, *The Emerald Isle,* by Sir Arthur Sullivan and Edward German. Featuring the well-known musical comedy actor Jefferson DeAngelis as Professor Bunn, an English confidence man, the show focused on the courtship of Lady Rosie Pippin, the daughter of the Lord Lieutenant of Ireland, by an Irish rebel named Terence O'Brian. There was not much public interest in the rather lackluster production, which ran for only a short time. But the failure was probably less important than the prestige which came from producing a show by one of England's foremost composers—and to Sam at any rate, prestige was a matter of some importance.

Clearly it was Sam, more than either of his brothers, who was the driving force behind the rapid Shubert expansion in the early years of the century. Lee seemed content at the time to follow his brother's lead, and J.J., truculent and unpredictable, was relegated mostly to handling out-of-town matters and to a less than full partnership in the growing company. Sam's health, however, gave his brothers some cause for anxiety, as the strain of almost constant work and travel began to undermine his already delicate constitution.

Little more than five feet tall, slim, and rather ascetically handsome, Sam was obviously possessed of considerable charm—a quality not often ascribed to either of his brothers. A 1909 article in the Shuberts' newspaper, the *New York Review,* contained an interesting

Two views of the Casino Theatre around the turn of the century. The Casino was designed as a home for light comedies, musical entertainments, balls, concerts, and lectures. The structure contained, among other amenities, a roof garden for summer entertainments, which became a popular Broadway gathering place in the eighties and nineties. The summer venue seems to have been virtually unused by Lee and J.J., however, who may not have found it profitable, although they did operate roof gardens at several of their other houses.

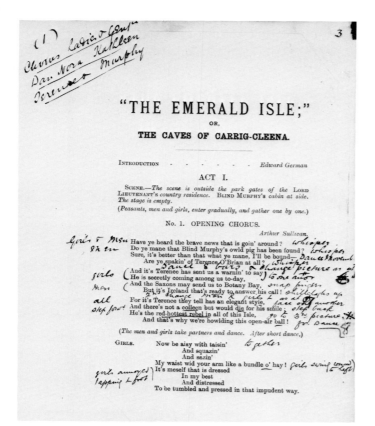

A page from the prompt-book of The Emerald Isle by Sir Arthur Sullivan and Edward German; and a costume design for the show. Jefferson De Angelis, the star of The Emerald Isle, was a musical comedy clown in the tradition of Thomas Q. Seabrook and De Wolf Hopper. De Angelis was immensely popular at the time, but his comic capers could not save the uninspired show. The Shuberts would use him again, however, in their highly successful 1905 production of Fantana and, in 1907, in The Gay White Way. A decade later, De Angelis and Hopper would join forces in J.J. Shubert's Passing Show of 1917.

description of Sam's striking physical appearance. After the usual generalizations about his "remarkable magnetism," the reporter recalled that Sam was "very slight and of very short stature, and wonderfully rapid in all his movements. It has been said of him that he never walked but always ran, as if trying to keep physical pace with his schemes and ambitions. His oval face was illuminated by his noticeably black eyes which were at once objectively penetrating and subjectively introspective. However far and hurriedly he traveled, his attire was invariable immaculate."

Although Sam never drank, the article went on to say that he "smoked almost without pause, consuming vast numbers of long, thin cigarettes prepared especially for his use. In his business office he was an absolute marvel of activity and gave personal attention to immense amounts of detail. He dictated with lightning rapidity, shifting from one matter to another with such amazing celerity that only one special private secretary, familiar with the intricacies of his affairs and remarkable for his speed as a stenographer, could ever successfully 'take him.'" But Sam's tremendous "nervous activity was a continual strain. Twice the New York newspapers put the 'dead watch' on him."

An ardent Anglophile, Sam was very much involved with importing London shows to Broadway and passionately interested in the possibility of establishing a Shubert chain in England. He seems to have left nothing to chance. Sam wrote constantly to his brothers about even the smallest business matters, and he shrewdly analyzed their chances for success in the light of every eventuality. About a proposed 1902 show, for example, Sam wrote to Lee in meticulous detail. "Also see [Lulu] Glaser and see if she agrees to appear in it, as without her in it, I would not give two cents for the piece." But he warned Lee that Glaser, a musical star of the day, was "a flighty young lady" who was "liable to change her mind, after saying she will go in it." Sam urged Lee to make a deal with the owners of a theatre in which he hoped to present the show, so "that if the thing is a failure, we have the right to cancel our theatre contract with them by giving them two weeks' notice." Lee was also to find out the seating capacity of the theatre "and what expense the attraction will be and see if the gamble is worth while taking the chance." Sam warned his brother not to "act hastily in this matter" and to remember that if the venture "is a success we will make a lot of money, if it is a failure we stand to lose a lot."

Sam was a ladies' man of some consequence, who established liaisons with—among others—Glaser and the vaudeville star Fay Templeton, and probably with Evelyn Nesbit, the infamous "Girl in the Red Velvet Swing," whose husband Harry Thaw murdered her lover, the architect Stanford White. Nesbit once wrote to Sam that she was sick ("it is to urrp!!!") and unable to meet him that night, urging him "to be good & do nothing wrong till you see—Evelyn. Sammy! oh—oh—oh Sammy! tra la la! I'll write you *huge* letters from Bosting."

Not long before his death, Sam established Templeton in a house on West Seventy-second Street and moved in his mother and sisters Sarah and Dora (by now his sister Fanny had married a Syracuse hardware merchant named Isaac Isaacs). For six months the Shubert women were coached by tutors to bring them up to New York social standards; they were then moved into their own home in the elegant Ansonia apartments on Broadway and Seventy-fourth Street. David remained in Syracuse, boarded out in the house of the family's onetime rabbi.

Sam's growing success had become a matter of some concern to the Syndicate, which now began to launch an all-out attack on this new threat to their theatre monopoly. Lee later pointed out that Sam "was tolerated as long as he stayed in line and let the Syndicate do his bookings and paid the Syndicate price. He would never be a menace. How could he when they had the power and the money? He had neither." In August 1903, however, Erlanger had second thoughts. He informed the Shuberts that they had broken a booking agreement by refusing a Syndicate attraction at a Shubert theatre in Chicago, and that they were finished in the theatre world. It was then that the theatrical wars began in earnest.

Borrowing a catch phrase from the recent Boxer Rebellion, Sam called for an "Open Door Policy" in the theatre and began a shrewd and highly systematic press war against the Syndicate, labeling the organization an enemy of both art and free enterprise. He did not lack listeners. The basis of Sam's policy is reiterated in a 1908 letter in *The Saturday Evening Post,* attributed to J.J. but almost certainly a

Sam Shubert on shipboard with unidentified friends (the woman may be Sam's lover, Fay Templeton); Lulu Glaser; and Evelyn Nesbit. Glaser, another of Sam's lovers, was a particular nemesis of Lee's. After one of his company managers complained that she was "unbearable," "a hopeless case," and "continually on the war path," he banned her from appearing in Shubert shows. Nesbit, who was probably also romantically involved with Sam, married the unstable Pennsylvania millionaire Harry K. Thaw, who later murdered society architect Stanford White.

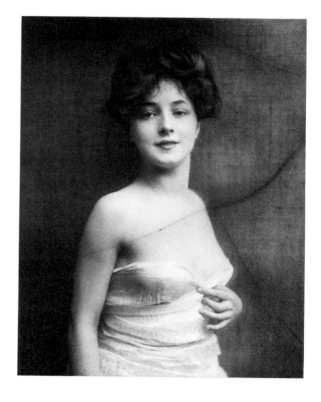

A photograph and a caricature of Abraham Erlanger. Erlanger was the pivotal figure in the Theatrical Syndicate and, for many years, the Shuberts' chief antagonist. Actors bitterly resented Erlanger's policies—but they found Lee and J.J. scarcely more enlightened. In his 1924 autobiography, actor Francis Wilson compared the profession's views of the two organizations. "The Syndicate," he wrote, "paid what it pleased, when it pleased, and where it pleased. . . . [The Shuberts] were no better and, in some respects, worse." The friction between performers and the ranking managers would lead ultimately to the formation of Actors' Equity in 1913 and to the famous Actors' Strike of 1919.

product of the Shubert press office. "The strength of our position," the letter reads, "in no way defers us from the principle of our contention—and that is, that every theatre should be free to play any attraction that its clientele desires. We want the open door, and we are going to strive for it until an indignant public shall swing it open despite the restraining influence of the Syndicate. Competition makes business; so let us have a clear field and no favor. New blood means new energy, and this is an energetic world wherein no man or corporation has a right to dictate the destiny of the theatre."

There is no question that the Syndicate's head, Abraham Erlanger, had many enemies in the theatre. He was eccentric, perhaps a touch mad, and certainly a terrifying character. P. G. Wodehouse and Guy Bolton, who worked for Erlanger early in their careers, referred to him in *Bring on the Girls* as "a bit of a Tartar. That's our expression. The Tartars, meeting a particularly tough specimen, would say that he was a bit of an Erlanger." Lee's view of his rival was, on the whole, not very different from that of Wodehouse, Bolton, and most of his contemporaries. Erlanger saw himself, Lee said, "as the theatrical Napoleon . . . Pictures and statues of the Little Corporal adorned his office and his home, and he was inordinately proud of his collection of Napoleonia which he bragged about and exhibited on every possible occasion. Frequently in his office he would strike a Napoleonic pose, with hands behind his back, feet spread apart, and a brooding scowl upon his face. The edicts he thundered forth from such an attitude had a fateful tone and always had the deeply impressive effect intended upon the visitor for whose benefit the show was put on. . . . Those who knew Erlanger best felt that his delusion of grandeur and invincibility was an almost pathological obsession." Now Erlanger moved swiftly to retaliate.

The pages of the Syndicate-controlled sporting and theatrical paper, *The Morning Telegraph*, were soon filled with anti-Shubert stories and editorials. The Shuberts responded by withdrawing their advertising and, in 1905, by creating a small magazine, *The Show*, to present theatrical news from the Shubert point of view. Meanwhile, the fledgling company was gaining financial strength and important allies among the independent producers whose lives had been made miserable by the Syndicate. Prominent among those allies were David

Photograph of producer David Belasco; and a caricature of Belasco and Abraham Erlanger. Belasco was an important early Shubert ally and a bitter enemy of the Theatrical Syndicate. In 1909, however, Belasco announced to the press that he and the Syndicate had found that they could "enter upon business relations for the betterment of the American stage without any sacrifice of principle, dignity or integrity."

Belasco, Harrison Grey Fiske, editor of *The New York Dramatic Mirror,* and his wife, actress Minnie Maddern Fiske.

Belasco, the flamboyant playwright-director-producer, had been a particular hero of Sam's since Syracuse days, and, like everyone else, he was genuinely fond of Sam. According to Belasco's biographer, critic William Winter, his subject told him that Sam, had he not died young, would have "'occupied a great place in the history of the

American theatre. He had keen business instincts, a lovable nature, and was the soul of honor.'" (Relations between Sam's brothers and Belasco would become strained in later years and by 1909 the director had swallowed his pride and allied himself with the Syndicate; Lee and J.J. would never forgive him.) The Fiskes were implacable enemies of the Syndicate. Mrs. Fiske, in fact, had appeared in skating rinks and churches and other makeshift theatres rather than sacrifice her independence for bookings in Syndicate houses. Her ploy was one which the Shuberts would shortly adopt for their own purposes, with highly satisfying results.

At the same time, the Shuberts were accumulating more theatres around the country. During 1904 and 1905, they were to gain leases on first-class houses in Buffalo, Baltimore, Brooklyn, Cleveland, Milwaukee, Chattanooga, and New Orleans. Where it was not possible to lease good theatres, the brothers began to build them, pulling in outside capital in the process. Their approach was far more liberal and expansive than that of the Syndicate, which tended to avoid construction whenever possible and to frown on outside financing. But by taking risks and spending money freely, Sam and Lee had acquired a string of some fifty theatres by the summer of 1904. About two-thirds of them were owned by the Shuberts or their backers; the rest were controlled by Shubert allies but booked by the brothers. By the spring of 1905 they employed some 1500 people and carried a weekly payroll of $75,000—not in the Syndicate's league, but no small sum at the turn of the century. Their company—Sam S. and Lee Shubert, Incorporated—had been formed the previous year with a capital of $1,400,000. Significantly, J.J.'s name did not appear on the company's letterhead.

By now Sam and Lee were starting to bring in a string of popular successes. One of these was *Fantana*, a musical farce, for which Sam supplied an idea developed by Robert B. Smith, a professional lyricist. The music was by Raymond Hubbell, a minor composer of the day. *Fantana*, which opened at the Lyric in January of 1905, was another of Sam's excursions to the exotic Orient, and it turned out to be a major hit of the 1904–1905 season. This time the plot centered on a retired naval commander and his daughter Fanny, nicknamed Fantana, who are to accompany the Japanese ambassador on a trip to

The cover of an early Shubert publication, The Show, *featuring a toast to Sam's production of* Fantana; *and a photograph of three of the show's performers, Katie Barry, Adele Ritchie, and Jefferson De Angelis. Sam was billed as the co-author of the script, and it seems likely that he had aspirations as a playwright. Over the years, J.J. would become something of a stage director manqué, but Lee seems to have had virtually no interest in the artistic side of show business except as a producer.*

his homeland. Fantana is in love with Sinclair, a naval officer, but her father insists that she marry a French count named Pasdoit. The ambassador is recalled to Washington, and Fantana gets her father's valet Hawkins to impersonate him. Sinclair turns up in Japan, Hawkins exposes the count as a fraud, and all ends happily, after Hawkins is almost beheaded by the Japanese.

In December of 1904, Sam and Lee—now billing themselves collectively as the "Messrs." Shubert—had produced a plush Lillian Russell musical, *Lady Teazle*. The show, based on *School for Scandal*, the famous eighteenth-century comedy by Richard Brinsley Sheridan, seemed to have enormous potential. But in spite of a well-known star, an elaborate production, and some eighty-six chorus

Front and rear of an advertising card for Lady Teazle. *Gaining Lillian Russell as one of their stars was an important step forward for the Shuberts. Although much of her career was behind her by 1904, when she appeared in the Shuberts' show, Russell was a legendary figure of the American stage. A decade later Lee and J.J. would produce a film version of her 1907 stage success* Wildfire *at their World Film studio in New Jersey.*

Lillian Russell
in "Lady Teazle"

At Home
Casino Theatre

girls, *Lady Teazle* did not attract much critical or popular interest and closed in less than two months. It was clear, however, that the Shuberts were continuing to raise their sights in terms of the stars they employed. During a lull in the Shubert-Syndicate wars in February of 1905, Sam presented the famous Irish-American comedienne Ada Rehan in repertory at the Liberty Theatre, a new Forty-second Street house built by Klaw and Erlanger as a home for the Rogers Brothers, a popular comedy team of the day. Rehan had been a long-time member of the famous stock company managed by Augustin Daly and a star of classic comedy. Although she was at the end of her career, her name was still important in both New York and London, and Sam featured her in several of her most famous roles.

At the same time, Sam was concluding arrangements to open the Waldorf (known today as the Strand), a London theatre he and Lee had recently leased. His opening attractions were to be world class; Eleonora Duse, the great Italian tragedienne, would alternate performances with the famous soprano Emma Calvé. As Sam conceived it, the Waldorf would become the flagship house for the Shuberts' English producing operation. A successful opening was vital. Suddenly, negotiations with the two stars broke down and Lee was sent to London to untangle the situation. A few days later Sam was dead.

II
MOVING ON

*After his sudden passing, J.J. and I solemnly
resolved to dedicate our lives to carrying out
his purpose, to bringing his dream to complete
reality . . . The victory, when it came, was his.*
LEE SHUBERT
On Sam's death

On the evening of May 11, 1905, Sam was on his way to Pittsburgh to
attend a hearing about a local theatre, the Duquesne, on which the
Shuberts once held a lease. They were now trying to win the house
back, and their competition was the Syndicate. With Sam was his
lawyer, William Klein, and Abe Thalheimer, the Shuberts' chief
booker. As the train sped down the track near Harrisburg, Pennsylvania, about 1:30 a.m. on the twelfth, it sideswiped a work train
parked on an adjacent siding which carried a car filled with blasting
powder. Twenty-two people died as a result of the explosion, among
them Sam Shubert.

J.J. managed to arrive in Harrisburg in time to hear Sam's last
words. One version of the story has Sam praising the bravery of
Thalheimer, who had pulled both of his companions from the wreck.
In another account, Sam died with an indictment of Erlanger on his
lips, telling J.J. to let Lee know that his rival had murdered him as
surely as if he had shot him to death.

His brothers were devastated at the loss. Lee seems to have been
particularly grief-stricken; still in London and unable to attend the
funeral held two days later, he appears to have had some sort of

SAM S. SHUBERT DIES OF INJURIES

Theatrical Manager Passed Away at Harrisburg.

BURNS CAUSED HIS DEATH

Father and Friends Informed of Sad Occurrence by The Herald.

SUCCESSFUL BUSINESS CAREER

WITHOUT ADVANTAGES HE BECAME AT 29 ONE OF THE LEADERS IN THE THEATRICAL WORLD.

At Least Twenty-one Lives Lost in the Pennsylvania Wreck—Several Persons Reported as Missing or as in a Critical Condition.

(Incidents of the wreck on page 17.)

[SPECIAL TO THE HERALD.]

HARRISBURG, Pa., May 12.—Sam S. Shubert of Syracuse and the head of the theatrical firm of Shubert Brothers, died here at 9:50 o'clock this morning as the result of injuries received in the Pennsylvania railroad horror of Wednesday night. The end occurred at the Commonwealth hotel, where Mr. Shubert was taken soon after his escape from the burning wreck on the shoulders of Abe Thalheimer. His mother, two sisters and his brother, Jacob J. Shubert, were at his bedside when death came. The family physician, Dr. O. M. Leiser of New York, who hastened to Harrisburg with a trained nurse, immediately upon learning of the catastrophe, and Solomon Thalheimer of New York, a friend, were also present.

Mr. Shubert's injuries were much more severe than was at first reported. While he was badly burned about the legs and body, the shock and the exposure while lying without clothing in the woods near the scene of the accident, contributed to the fatal result. Doctor Leiser, upon his arrival, considered the case so serious that he wired for the family to come on at once.

Abe Thalheimer and William Klein, the lawyer who was accompanying Mr. Shubert to Pittsburg to close the lease of the Duquesne theater, have almost entirely recovered from their injuries and will accompany the body to New York this afternoon.

Sam Shubert's obituary from the Syracuse, (New York) Herald, May 12, 1905; and a notation from the company's letter copy book at the time of Sam's death. The obituary comes from a scrapbook found among Lee and J.J.'s papers, which contains dozens of newspaper articles that appeared around the country in the days following the fatal accident. Sam's brothers also saved hundreds of letters and telegrams of condolence, among them one from a London acquaintance of Sam's who noted that "I shall not easily forget the charm of his unaffected simplicity and the friendly generous tenour of the way he treated business negotiations."

breakdown and possibly to have attempted suicide. It was rumored that he and J.J. were so dispirited that they would shortly sell out to Klaw and Erlanger. Clearly, Erlanger realized that grief and confusion had placed the surviving Shubert brothers in a weak position. But, in fact, Lee and J.J. were making no concessions, and within a few weeks of Sam's death they had launched an aggressive expansion program. Soon they gained control of the fateful Duquesne, along with theatres in Newark and Cleveland, and shortly they began construction of new houses in Cincinnati and Kansas City.

In addition, as Lee wrote, "we had made booking arrangements with the Providence Opera House, the Hyperion Theatre in New Haven, the Auditorium Theatre in Baltimore, the Garrick Theatre in Detroit, the Lyric in Cincinnati, the Valencia in San Francisco, the Alhambra in Seattle, the Shubert in Portland, the Auditorium in Los Angeles, the Grand in Salt Lake City, the Princess in Montreal, the Murat in Indianapolis, the Alhambra in Milwaukee." They also "purchased the newly built Royal Theatre in Kansas City. The latter was the first of several new houses that we built as memorials to our departed brother."

One of Sam's theatres, the Waldorf, turned out to be an unmitigated disaster. As Lee tells it, the Shuberts found that "competing in grand opera with Covent Garden, even with a company of celebrated stars, was a hazardous thing to do." Equally hazardous, it appeared, was producing Duse in London. A few years later Morris Gest would present her at the Metropolitan Opera in New York to receipts of $12,000 a night; in London, no one seemed interested. Lee wrote that the great tragic actress played to "row upon row of empty seats!! Or it would have been so if we had not 'papered' the house. Receipts as little as eleven, twelve and thirteen pounds a performance!!"

Julia Marlowe and E.H. Sothern, the husband and wife team famous for their Shakespearean roles, fared better at the Waldorf. But the English could not really understand the Shuberts' approach to publicity. Lee recalled that the "screaming newspaper advertisements, and gaudy street displays, which really were no more flaming than American cities regularly were accustomed to, the parade of sandwich men down Piccadilly and the Strand, caused conservative Britishers to stare amazedly and, of course, to write letters to the

Times." In fact, the uninhibited publicity campaign worked to some extent, but not enough to turn the theatre into a profitable operation. J.J. would later write to Lee that the venture was a dead loss: "I tell you this house could not be given away for taxes alone without rent."

The Shuberts never really understood theatre management as practised by the English because it was diametrically opposed to their own methods. In 1912, Lee would write from London with a certain wry amusement that he had found that it was "impossible to do anything quick in this country as they are so slow. They go away for three days at the end of the week, and when they are in town they are only in the office for an hour or two." Yet, he pointed out, "they know how to live and get as much out of it as we do."

Lee and J.J. continued to produce on Broadway, including several of Sam's imports in their 1905–1906 season. Among them was an Ivan Caryll musical called *The Earl and the Girl.* Caryll was a Belgian composer whose shows were frequently seen in England and the United States at the turn of the century. His *The Earl and the Girl,* produced at the Casino in November of 1905, starred the popular comedian Eddie Foy as a dog trainer who switches places with a nobleman so that the peer can court an American heiress. Lee later noted that Foy, who appeared in a number of Shubert shows over the years, "could pull a tantrum on a short notice and for as little reason as any leading soprano in grand opera," generally illustrating his displeasure by "the simple expedient of throwing his costumes into a trunk, dragging the trunk through the stage door to the sidewalk and hailing a cab" ten minutes before curtain time.

Foy's temperament was almost certainly matched by J.J. Shubert's. Sam's death had finally brought J.J. into New York and firmly into the center of the business. But it was money, not brotherly affection, that carried J.J. to Broadway. William Klein explained the matter in his lawyerly prose in a brief reminiscence about the early days of the Shuberts. "After Sam Shubert died," he said, "a third brother Jacob J. Shubert, who held forth in Rochester, came to New York. Lee Shubert needed money to continue and had very little. Jacob J. Shubert had in the savings bank upstate about seventy thousand dollars, and he brought this down to New York with him and it was used as capital along with such other moneys as Lee Shubert had."

The Shubert Theatre, Kansas City, Missouri, 1909; one of the many Shubert houses around the country. In the years following Sam's death, Lee and J.J. launched an aggressive expansion program. As J.J.'s son John explained it, by the 1910–11 season, "the Shuberts owned seventy-three theatres outright and held booking contracts with many more. They possessed more than fifty dramatic and musical companies. All in all, the brothers had come a long way since the spring of 1905, when they made the decision to carry on the burdens of their theatrical interests despite Sam's death."

Sometime in 1906—perhaps—J.J. met a young Irish Catholic schoolgirl named Catherine Dealy, who claimed to have been a student at the Manhattanville Convent of the Sacred Heart in Harlem, although there is no record of her attendance there. According to one version of the story, Catherine and J.J. eloped and were married in a civil ceremony in the spring of 1906 at the Shubert offices above the Lyric Theatre, only cabling her family when they were headed out to sea for a European honeymoon. Another version has the pair married in 1907 in Rheims, France. In December 1908, Catherine and J.J.'s only child, John, was born at the couple's new home on Seventy-first Street and West End Avenue.

J.J. neglected to tell Lee about his marriage for some time. The reason seemingly lay in a pact between the two—which J.J. had ignored—not to marry without the other's permission. The logic, apparently, was to avoid the possibility of a surviving widow ever becoming involved with the company. This may well have been so; certainly, through the years, Lee and J.J. jealously guarded their almost total control over every aspect of the company's operation. They shared real power only with each other—and then reluctantly—although family did become involved with the lower echelons of the business. In 1909, for example, Dora Shubert, Lee and J.J.'s sister, married a Texan named Milton Wolf, who would be connected with the company for many years, running Joseph's, a retail women's store which also produced Shubert costumes.

At Sam's death it was Lee, a complex and difficult character, who emerged as the acknowledged leader of the Shubert theatrical enterprise. Like Sam, Lee turned out to be an immensely talented business strategist and a compulsive worker, who thought nothing of a twelve-

Sam Shubert's Waldorf Theatre, London. One of a series of photographs, circa 1905, showing details of the elaborate auditorium decor in what was described as "the Louis XIV style." After Lee and J.J.'s disastrous experience as managers of the house, it was taken over briefly by another American manager, F. C. Whitney, who gave it his name. The theatre, renamed the Strand in 1910, was badly damaged during the bombing of London in 1940, but it has survived to the present day with a much modified auditorium.

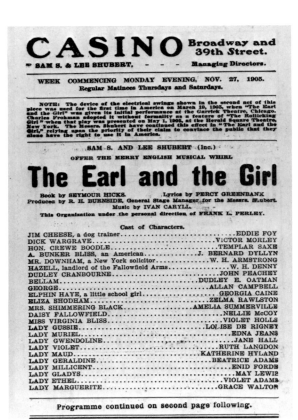

Program for The Earl and the Girl *at the Casino Theatre, 1905. Lee found comic actor Eddie Foy, who was featured in the play as Jim Cheese, to be difficult and temperamental. Perhaps the feeling was mutual; in any case, Foy's onstage personality was of a quite different order. As a critic once noted about him in the* Dramatic Mirror: *"Eddie Foy is the mildest, least obtrusive comedian on the stage. His is the art that conceals art. . . . If he exaggerates any personal trait, it is that air of open-eyed and wondering innocence that sits so well upon him, suggesting a Rip Van Winkle after a few days' wandering on Broadway."*

or fifteen-hour day and a seven-day week. He was also painfully shy and probably only semi-literate. He chose to cover up feelings of inadequacy and embarrassment with an icy and, to some, rather menacing politeness. The effect was formidable, and in later years Lee's increasingly chilly demeanor, combined with his hawk-like features and a more-or-less permanent mahogany suntan, would earn him the not altogether affectionate nickname of The Wooden Indian.

Yet, from the beginning, it was Lee who was the public figure and the one to be taken seriously by others in the theatre. A dinner in his honor was held in 1908 by the Friars, a theatrical club founded a few years earlier by press agents. (The head of the Shubert press office was a prominent member and served on the dinner committee.) J.J. is never even mentioned in the program; Lee's accomplishments, however, are trumpeted in a number of cartoons. In one of them Syracuse is seen in the background, with a road leading from it to New York. Lee sits astride the Casino Theatre in the foreground, his hands and his lap filled with other theatre buildings. In another drawing he is shown as a magician, conjuring up the names of the company's most popular stars and most successful shows out of a top hat labeled "Nerve and Ability." In a third cartoon Lee appears as a mahout, riding an elephant labeled with the name of a recently acquired Shubert theatre, the Hippodrome. The elephant draws "Lee Shubert's N.Y. Band Wagon," which is filled with the Shubert stars of the day. Among the speakers at the dinner were such luminaries as Augustus Thomas, Otis Skinner, Harrison Grey Fiske, James K. Hackett, Lew Fields, and Sam Bernard—all identified with the Shubert camp in the war against the Syndicate.

J.J. was seemingly less complicated than Lee, but even more intimidating. Pugnacious, stubborn, naïve, and inclined to physical violence when crossed, he seems not to have had the complete confidence of Sam or Lee, neither of whom ever granted him full

J.J.'s first wife, Catherine Dealy Shubert, Pasadena, California, 1910. As John Shubert reconstructed it, his parents first met at a matinee in a Shubert theatre. "My mother remembers the day vividly. 'Your father and I met,' she would often say in an unruffled voice, 'in the rear of the Lyric auditorium between the water fountain and a coiled fire hose.'" The relationship was complex from the outset, and neither family seems to have approved. After their marriage, John noted, the Dealeys "hung a banner of black crepe around the front door of their Harlem apartment, where it remained for the next two years."

Cartoon from the program for a dinner in honor of Lee Shubert, the Friars, 1908. In his history of the Friars, which was founded by press agents, Joey Adams points to the origins of what would later become the club's famous "roasts." The press agents, Adams says, "ever itchy to find another way to scratch their clients' egos and always looking for a new promotional angle, came up with the idea of a guest-of-honor dinner. They kicked off a series of dinners to noted men, principally within the theatrical profession and principally their paid-up clients. This method of garnering publicity for their customers was coincidentally doing the same thing for the club."

participation in company policy or business decisions. John says that it was not until 1907 that the firm's name was changed—at J.J.'s violent insistence—from "Sam S. and Lee Shubert Enterprises" to "Lee and J.J. Shubert Enterprises." As John tells it, "Father, in an enormous rage, had charged like a rhinoceros into Lee's office, swinging his arms in all directions, demanding corporate recognition. The frightened Lee quickly ducked out of the building and found some excuse to remain in absentia until all Shubert signs and stationery included J.J.'s name." (In fact, stationery from the 1920s was still headed "Sam S. & Lee Shubert Inc.")

The perpetual backseat into which his brothers propelled him did not help J.J.'s disposition. After Sam's death, he engaged in a kind of on-going brushfire warfare with Lee which became a Broadway legend. According to John, "There was never rivalry between the two brothers in regard to bank accounts, real estate, or legal problems.

But producing a show was something else again." The two men finally came to avoid face-to-face confrontations as too painful and unproductive and carried on many of their negotiations through messengers
who shuttled back and forth between their offices. Yet they could
cooperate quite harmoniously where a vital business deal was concerned, and together they created an effective and—to many people
on Broadway—quite terrifying team.

As Lee and J.J. expanded the company's operations after Sam's
death, they were also mustering their forces to create a direct challenge to the Syndicate. Among their other ploys, they created the
Society of Independent Managers, an anti-Syndicate cabal made up of
such old hands as Belasco and the Fiskes. The Shuberts also announced that they had booked the great French tragedienne Sarah
Bernhardt for a farewell tour of the United States in 1906. It was
around Bernhardt's tour that Erlanger made his stand—and it proved
a disastrous one. All across the continent Syndicate theatres were
closed to the star. Taking a leaf from Mrs. Fiske's book, the Shuberts
rented a circus tent for Bernhardt's performances. The tent proved a
shrewd public relations device which gained the tour and its producers acres of free newspaper coverage, most of which cast the

*Sarah Bernhardt in front of the tent in which she performed while on tour for
the Shuberts in 1906, as a result of being shut out of Theatrical Syndicate
houses; and a 1909 cartoon attacking the Syndicate during the so-called
Theatrical Wars, which Lee and J.J., as leaders of the Independent Movement
in the theatre, waged with Abraham Erlanger and his associates. As historian
Arthur Hornblow would point out in 1919, "Cities that could support but one
first-class theatre were compelled to have two—a Syndicate theatre and an
Independent theatre. . . . Fierce competition resulted in overproduction and
a superfluity of theatres."*

Syndicate in a decidedly villainous role. As a result, the six Syndicate members were indicted by a New York grand jury for conspiracy to restrain trade, and Lee cheerfully testified at the hearings.

The indictment was dismissed, but relations between the Shuberts and the Syndicate had reached a particularly low ebb. Within a short time, however, there was a surprising turn about. Erlanger had become interested in getting into the lucrative vaudeville business, which was dominated at the time by B. F. Keith's United Booking Office in much the same way that the Syndicate dominated legitimate theatre activity. Erlanger conceived of a new operation called "Advanced Vaudeville" to challenge Keith, but he soon found that he needed more theatres to compete effectively. The obvious, if somewhat galling, answer was to approach Lee and J.J., who by now controlled a number of large houses suitable for vaudeville.

As a result, in 1907, Erlanger joined with his old enemies to form the United States Amusement Company, a vaudeville chain in direct competition with the UBO. Their bookings were handled by the talented young William Morris, who would later become a major theatrical agent. Included were such important stars as the Scottish comedian Harry Lauder and the great English music hall star Vesta Victoria. But their competitor was too skilled and too knowledgeable about the vaudeville business; by 1908 the combined Shubert-Syndicate circuit had been sold to Keith—at an attractive profit—and the Shuberts had signed an agreement not to enter vaudeville for another ten years.

Lee and J.J. were still buying, building, and leasing theatres in the Northeast and the Middle West. They now controlled houses in Hartford, Springfield, Willimantic, Northampton, and Toledo, and were building a new theatre in Sioux City. Between 1905 and 1911, the Shuberts were also leasing and building theatres all over New York City. They took leases on Daly's at Broadway and Thirtieth Street, the Broadway at Forty-first Street, the Majestic near Columbus Circle, and the fantastic Hippodrome on Sixth Avenue. They built the Nazimova and Maxine Elliott's Theatre on Thirty-ninth Street, the Comedy on Forty-first Street, and four uptown theatres, the West End at One Hundred and Twenty-fifth Street, the Metropolis in the Bronx, the Yorkville on East Eighty-sixth Street, and the Lincoln Square on Broadway at Sixty-seventh Street.

In 1908 Lee had built a handsome small theatre in partnership with his star Maxine Elliott. The theatre, which bore Elliott's name, stood on Thirty-ninth Street, between Sixth Avenue and Broadway, and was designed by Ben Marshall, a Chicago architect. Lee and J.J. continued to produce in the house as late as 1917, but it was abundantly clear by then that it had no real place in their expansion plans, which now were centering on Forty-fourth and Forty-fifth streets. They did, however, hold on to another small Thirty-ninth Street house until the mid-twenties. Alla Nazimova was an important Shubert attraction in 1910 when the theatre bearing her name was built just a few doors away from Maxine Elliott's Theatre. The small house, designed by William Swasey and known as the Thirty-ninth Street Theatre after Nazimova's defection to another manager, never attracted much attention and was replaced by an office building in 1926.

In 1909, Lee and J.J. opened a third small house, the Comedy Theatre, two blocks to the north on Forty-first Street between Sixth Avenue and Broadway. Designed by D. G. Malcolm, it was used for a number of small-scale Shubert productions through the mid-twenties, including, in 1911, the immensely popular *Bunty Pulls the Strings,* an import from London's Haymarket Theatre about rural Scottish life. The Comedy was often rented out to other producers, among them the Washington Square Players, progenitor of the Theatre Guild, which later presented a number of important plays at the house, including Eugene O'Neill's *In the Zone.*

Perhaps the Shuberts' most unusual venture into theatre real estate had come earlier, in 1906, when, with producer Max Anderson, they took a fifteen-year lease on the New York Hippodrome for a quarter of a million dollars. The 5000-seat Hippodrome, on Sixth Avenue between Forty-third and Forty-fourth streets, had been built in the previous year by Frederic Thompson and Elmer "Skip" Dundy, the creators of Coney Island's famous pleasure resort, Luna Park. The gigantic theatre—more than four times the size of a standard Broadway house—was almost immediately in deep financial trouble, and Thompson and Dundy were delighted to unload their white elephant on the Shubert brothers. Lee and J.J., however, were convinced that the Hippodrome could be turned into a money-making operation.

In September 1906, the Shuberts restaged a Thompson-Dundy spectacle from the previous season, *A Society Circus.* By November,

Maxine Elliott's Theatre and the star in her dressing room. Now virtually forgotten, Elliott was a major performer in both England and America in the years before World War I, and the sometime wife of an equally famous star, Nat Goodwin. A Chicago newspaper noted in 1909 that she was "the owner and manager of the only theater in America conducted by a woman—the Maxine Elliott, a little playhouse situated in Thirty-ninth street, just off Broadway." The information suggests the hand of the Shubert press office; in fact, she was not the only woman to operate an American theatre at the time, and she did not own the house—Lee and J.J., of course, possessed a controlling interest in it.

*Caricature of the Russian star Alla Nazimova by Howell, from the Shuberts'
theatrical newspaper,* The New York Review, *1909. Howell drew a series of
caricatures of Shubert stars, as well as a number of anti-Syndicate cartoons.
The Shuberts' contract with Nazimova specified that they would hire a language instructor for her and look after her "comfort and instruction" while
she "engaged in perfecting her knowledge of the English language" for a
period of seven months. Characteristically, the caption accompanying the
caricature claims that she did it in four.*

they had their own extravaganza in place, a triple bill called *Pioneer
Days*. The title piece was a three-act Western melodrama complete
with a full-scale battle between Indians and a troop of mounted caval-
ry. The melodrama was accompanied by a one-act circus and a so-
called "Operatic Extravaganza," *Neptune's Daughter,* which made
use of the theatre's much admired water tank. Located in the front of
the stage, the huge tank was basically a swimming pool fitted out with
a device that permitted chorus girls to disappear mysteriously at the
end of a number.

Lee recalled that he obtained the device—the "bell," as it was
called—from a shabby old man who came to see him at his office one
day. "I was greatly interested," Lee wrote, "but told him that it
would be necessary to see a practical working model." The model,
"made of wood, was constructed on the Hippodrome stage and when
completed was installed in the tank . . . When the compressed air
was turned into the bell it was blown to pieces and the little old man,
who was inside it, shot away up into the air and came down in the
water." The man survived, however, and the device became the Hippodrome's single most popular attraction.

The Shuberts were to continue to operate the house until 1915,
presenting a string of more-or-less similar extravaganzas with such
titles as *The Auto Race* (1907), *Under Many Flags* (1912), and *Wars of
the World* (1914). The Hippodrome was a profitable operation for a
time, but in later years it became a liability as the developing motion
picture industry drew away more and more of its audience. For a
while, in fact, the theatre offered a combined stage and film show of
the sort that was later to become famous at Radio City Music Hall.
But by 1915, the Shuberts, having written off the house as having no

ACT I. SCENE IN "THE INTERNATIONAL CUP"

ACT II. THE BABY NUMBER IN "THE INTERNATIONAL CUP"

THE BALLET OF "NIAGARA"

Scenes from the 1910 Shubert production of The International Cup *and* The Ballet of Niagara *at the Hippodrome; costume designs for three other Hippodrome shows:* The Battle of Port Arthur *(1908),* Neptune's Daughter *(1906), and* Sporting Days *(1908). The costume sketches are by Alfredo Edel, who worked at the Hippodrome for eight seasons. Edel was a specialist in spectacle costuming—what he called "that realm of the theatric art where the stage is crowded with people, especially with pretty girls clad in many-colored, brilliant garments of various sorts and designs." The irrepressible Shubert press office suggested that advertising for* The Ballet of Niagara *should ask readers the critical question: "Why make a trip to Niagara Falls, when you can see it at the Hippodrome?"*

potential for profit, had closed its doors. A press release noted that the "Messrs. Shubert are frank to state that their reason for not desiring to operate the Hippodrome any more is that the possibilities of this playhouse, from the standpoint of scenic surprises, have been exhausted." The huge theatre limped along under various producers for another two decades and was finally razed in 1939.

In the years after Sam's death, Lee and J.J. were, for the most part, presenting an untaxing collection of light plays, musical comedies, and operettas, with a sprinkling of more or less unprofitable serious plays. It was to become a familiar combination over the next few years. A typical Shubert Hippodrome show, *The Auto Race,* opened in November 1907. The show contained not only a spectacular race around the theatre's gigantic stage, but a naval engagement in the tank, a full-dress garden party, a ballet, and the by-now traditional circus segment. Playing twice a day, *The Auto Race* managed a run of more than 300 performances during the theatre season of 1907–1908.

In the 1907–1908 season the Shuberts were involved with an adaptation of Tolstoy's *Anna Karenina* and a production of Ibsen's *Master Builder,* with Alla Nazimova. But far more typical Shubert fare was *The Girl Behind the Counter,* an English musical retailored for the great comedian Lew Fields, formerly teamed with comic Joe Weber, and now beginning a relationship with the Shuberts—both as performer and producer—that would last for decades. Also typical fare was *The Gay White Way,* with the popular actor Jefferson De Angelis, who had appeared in Sam's *Fantana,* and vaudevillian Blanche Ring. Like many musical shows of the day, *The Gay White Way* was, strictly speaking, neither a revue nor a book musical. There was a semblance of a plot about the adventures of an amateur detective, but the story existed largely to frame sketches that parodied other Broadway shows.

During the season of 1907–1908, Lee and J.J. also produced *The Girls of Holland,* an overblown operetta by Reginald DeKoven, and *Nearly a Hero,* a modest musical, starring popular comedian Sam Bernard and Ethel Levey, the singer and comedienne, about a mysterious stranger who saves a matinee idol from drowning and a stage-struck girl who constantly imitates Ethel Barrymore. The book was by the Broadway perennial Harry B. Smith, who, over the years, worked for the Shuberts and virtually everyone else on Broadway, turning out librettos or lyrics for a hundred shows.

The Shuberts also mounted several unsuccessful straight plays and two popular successes, *The Wolf* by Eugene Walter, and *Girls* by Clyde Fitch, the author of *The City,* which Lee and J.J. would later produce in 1909 to packed houses. *Girls,* a comedy about three young women living in a New York City studio, was hardly among Fitch's most distinguished efforts; it ran for only eight weeks in New York, although it had a considerable road tour. Fitch's contemporary, Eugene Walter, was an extremely facile melodramatist whose work is totally forgotten today. *The Wolf,* billed by the Shuberts as "Walter's Greatest Play"—which it manifestly is not—was a fairly standard melodrama set in the Canadian woods, complete with wolf howls recorded at a local zoo. The play ran longer than *Girls* and would turn out to be highly successful on the road.

Two shows the Shuberts did *not* present during the season of 1907–1908 are worth a word or two as a preview of things to come. Producer Florenz Ziegfeld's *Follies,* the new summer revue which opened in 1907, was backed by Klaw and Erlanger. The *Follies* played the New York Theatre Roof, which Ziegfeld, attempting to stress the Continental flavor of his revue, renamed the Jardin de Paris. Other light, topical summer revues, often produced in open-air roof-top theatres, had been popular for more than a decade. The immensely talented Ziegfeld, however, added a special touch of theatricality and a chorus of fifty beautiful showgirls, which turned his *Follies* into a unique—and highly profitable—summer entertainment. It was so profitable, in fact, that Ziegfeld offered a second edition during the summer of 1908. Meanwhile, the Shuberts, who apparently loathed Ziegfeld almost as much as they did Klaw and Erlanger, were carefully observing the *Follies* formula and planning their own variation, the first of which was the unsuccessful *The Mimic World* of 1908. Later they were to refine their approach with *The Passing Show,* which they presented most summers from 1912 through the mid-twenties in direct competition with Ziegfeld.

The hit of the 1907–1908 season and a show that was to change the history of musical theatre in America was *The Merry Widow.* The

Lew Fields in "The Girl Behind the Counter"

Lew Fields   Connie Ediss   MR. FIELDS AND MISS EDISS AT THE SODA FOUNTAIN   Lew Fields   Connie Ediss

THE PONY BALLET

THE SIX STATELY SHOW GIRLS

Scenes from The Girl Behind the Counter, *with Lew Fields; and a sheet-music cover for a song from* The Gay White Way, *with Jefferson De Angelis. The two shows were Shubert successes in 1907, and both their stars had been established and extremely popular figures on Broadway for a number of years. Fields and his former partner Joe Weber were show business legends. Lewis Strang's* Celebrated Comedians of Light Opera and Musical Comedy in America, *published six years earlier, noted that De Angelis combined "the bubbling merriment of the comedian of temperament with the physical activity and eccentricity of the comedian devoted absolutely to the acrobatic school. . . . But Mr. De Angelis is much more than an acrobatic comedian. He is a character actor of genuine humor and uncommon skill."*

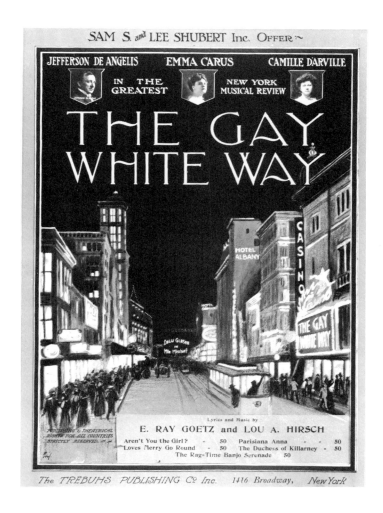

operetta by Franz Lehar had already had a successful European run when it opened in 1907 at the New Amsterdam, Erlanger's flagship theatre on Forty-second Street. The story about a rich widow who is courted by a prince because of her wealth, and later because of his genuine affection for her, was relatively straight-forward and coherent for a Viennese operetta of the day. But it was because of its fine score that *The Merry Widow* became a success, with a New York run of more than 400 performances and a number of profitable road companies. More than any other single musical, perhaps, it influenced the course of Lee and J.J.'s producing over the next twenty-five years. Like most other producers, they had been offering a mixed bag of traditional comic operas and the newer English revues and musical comedies. Now, as a result of *The Merry Widow,* the Shuberts—J.J. especially—began a passionate and highly lucrative involvement with

Sheet-music cover from The Mimic World (1908), an unsuccessful revue, produced by the Shuberts and Lew Fields on the model of Florenz Ziegfeld's highly esteemed Follies of the previous year. The story goes that Ziegfeld, already an enemy of the Shuberts, came close to suing the producers when he heard that they were planning to use the word "Follies" in the subtitle of their show. In fact, it appears that he managed to block its use until 1919, when a small-scale downtown revue called Greenwich Village Nights changed its title to Greenwich Village Follies. The revue, ironically, was moved to Broadway by the Shuberts, who presented it in a number of editions under its new title.

Advertising card for The Wolf, written by a former journalist, Eugene Walter, and produced by the Shuberts in 1908. Melodramas like The Wolf were very important to the Shuberts early in their producing careers. Plays by such popular writers of melodrama as Walter, George Broadhurst, and Charles Klein were often highly profitable, although they were almost universally scorned by "serious" critics and literary historians. Arthur Hobson Quinn wrote in his 1927 history of American drama that while such writers needed to be mentioned in his book on occasion, "usually their work has dropped below the level which requires our attention."

the world of operetta. Clearly, Erlanger could not go unchallenged. During the next season Lee and J.J. would produce two operettas; within two decades they would present dozens more, including such major hits as *Blossom Time, The Student Prince,* and *Maytime.*

If the Hippodrome had seemed at first to have some promise as a money-making operation, the New Theatre on Sixty-second Street and Central Park West was a failure from its very first day. Opened in November 1909 with Lee as general manager, it had been conceived by the distinguished producer Winthrop Ames as the home for an American repertory company on the model of the Moscow Art Theatre and the Comédie Française. The new playhouse was nicknamed the "Millionaires' Theatre" because of its rich and influential sponsors—including such luminaries as William K. Vanderbilt, J.P. Morgan, Otto Kahn, August Belmont, Harry Payne Whitney, and John Jacob Astor—some of whom were also on the board of directors of the Metropolitan Opera.

The theatre, which cost the then unheard of sum of three million dollars to construct, was outfitted with all of the latest stage equipment, including what Lee claimed was the first revolving stage in the country. The acoustics, however, were dreadful. Beyond that, the elegant Beaux-Arts building by the firm of Carrère and Hastings, architects of the New York Public Library at Fifth Avenue and Forty-second Street, was too far north of the theatre district, too large for straight plays (the mammoth auditorium seated 2300 spectators), and plagued by too many distinguished failures.

The New Theatre opened with much fanfare and a disastrous production of Shakespeare's *Antony and Cleopatra,* starring the famous acting team of Sothern and Marlowe. The experiment lurched along for two years with similarly high-minded—and largely unsought-after—fare. There were several more plays by Shakespeare, and works by such important contemporary writers as Edward Sheldon, John Galsworthy, and Arthur Wing Pinero. Far and away the most successful production was Maurice Maeterlinck's *The Bluebird,* a rather pretentious fairy tale-allegory which took New York by storm during the 1910–1911 season. Yet, even *The Bluebird,* as popular as it was, could not manage to make money.

The New Theatre, on Central Park West, in 1909. In 1926, the huge theatre, then known as the Century, would be the home to one of Lee and J.J.'s most eccentric productions, The Pearl of Great Price, *"A Driving, Smashing, Flaming Human Document" about virginity—or, more to the point, about losing it. The Shuberts press department attacked the publicity issue from every possible angle. The "drama-spectacle," with a cast of 200 and a symphony orchestra, was pitched in high-toned moral advertisements ("I am CHASTITY. I am the heritage of all womankind. . . . I am 'as pure as a pearl and as perfect; a noble and innocent girl.' I am THE PEARL OF GREAT PRICE."). Working the other side of the street, they also planted anonymous letters in the newspapers from supposedly shocked audience members.*

By the end of 1910, Ames and Lee were writing to the founders that they both believed that "in the present New Theatre building, dramatic attractions of the type contemplated by the founders cannot be presented with desirable results either financial or artistic." The only solution they saw was to turn the theatre over to comic opera and "high class visiting attractions from Europe." That is essentially what happened. In later years, the theatre passed through a number of hands. The producer George Tyler leased the house and renamed it the Century. After Tyler failed with several spectacular productions, it went to Charles Dillingham and Florenz Ziegfeld, and then to Morris Gest, who produced Max Reinhardt's *The Miracle* and several other Reinhardt spectacles in the house. Lee and J.J. eventually leased the Century themselves and finally bought it outright for $1,250,000, razing it in 1929 to build an apartment house, also known as the Century, which still stands on the site.

A scene from the 1910 production of Maeterlinck's The Bluebird *at the New Theatre. Reviewers in New York and on the road lavished praise on the play's poetry and its high moral tone. "Its story appeals to all the seven ages of man," wrote a Syracuse drama critic. "To the child it is a fairy tale; to the youth a spectacle; to maturity the symbolism of life, and to all an entertaining joy." Although the play has been largely forgotten today—some might say with good reason—*The Bluebird *was among the most prestigious productions with which the Shubert name had been connected up to that time.*

Curiously, the New Theatre fiasco had presented some distinct advantages to Lee. If the experiment was a failure, at least it was a prestigious one, and Lee's very connection with it suggested that he was being taken more seriously as a man of the theatre. Like Sam before him, Lee was anxious to build the image of the Shuberts as producers of "important" plays. Such plays usually lost money, but they almost certainly filled some need of Lee's for respectability. And they also served as a kind of memorial tribute to the superior taste and discernment which Sam had possessed in abundance and which Lee could only hope to imitate. J.J., on the other hand, was indifferent to art in the theatre on any terms except his own and was often

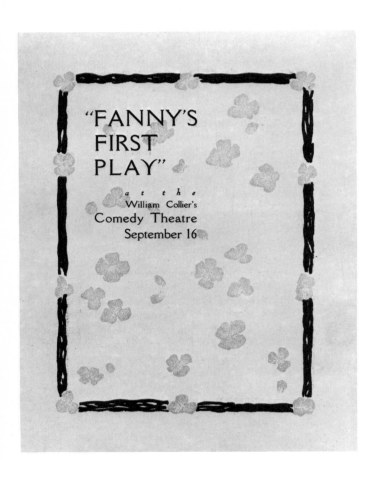

A program cover for the Shubert production of Shaw's Fanny's First Play (1912); and an invitation to the dress rehearsal. The play was a considerable success and, like The Bluebird two years earlier, evidence of Lee Shubert's sometime interest in producing plays by distinguished dramatists. But Shaw and Lee were obviously too unlikely a combination to succeed for long, and they never came to terms about any of Shaw's plays after 1912. Shaw once wrote to Lee about an aborted Shubert production of Pygmalion in which he had hoped to star Mrs. Patrick Campbell: "I did my best to bring the Pygmalion contract off; but the lady would not be persuaded that she could not make a better bargain. So she went ahead and made a worse one. Such is life. In great haste / ever / G. Bernard Shaw."

The Messrs. Shubert have the honor to request the pleasure of your company at the dress rehearsal of Granville Barker's company, in association with the Kingsway Theatre, London, in

"Fanny's First Play"

George Bernard Shaw's latest satire at the Comedy Theatre, Sunday Evening, September Fifteenth, at Eight-fifteen o'clock.

ADDRESS TELEGRAMS.
TO "SOCIALIST WESTRAND-LONDON"

10 ADELPHI TERRACE
LONDON W.C.

899

27th October 1915.

Dear Mr Lee Shubert

How did it all happen? As I understand it,
you made Miss Kingston an offer of $500 a week, and 25% of the
net profits. Miss Kingston then nailed you to your offer by
insisting on agreed expenses, which is the only way in which a
profit sharing agreement can be made effective. You then cried
off. What I dont understand is why you made such an offer. If
she had made such a demand I should have told her that it was too
much to load the plays with. But as it came from you, there was
nothing more to be said.

Have I got it right?

Yours faithfully

G. Bernard Shaw

You made her an offer of $500 weekly and 25% of net profits. She cabled back

$500 weekly and 25% of the GROSS RECEIPTS after first $4000, salary while

rehearsing

Lee Shubert Esq.,
Shubert Theatre Building
223 West 44th Street,
New York City

Letter from George Bernard Shaw to Lee Shubert, 1915, about a proposed Shubert production of two Shaw one-acters, Great Catherine *(which he had previously denied Lee the right to present) and a new play,* The Inca of Perusalem, *both to star the actress Gertrude Kingston. In an earlier letter to Lee, Shaw had outlined an elaborate scheme to keep the plot of* The Inca *secret and to hide his identity as its author until the opening. "Make a complete mystery of it," Shaw wrote. "If the slightest expectation is raised the result will be a disappointment and the discussion will be over before the curtain goes up, when it will be no use. The Inca must come on the first night as a surprise and a sensation. . . . The authorship will be obvious, but it must not be admitted." Lee was undoubtedly confused by the whole affair.*

hostile about "artistic" plays clearly doomed to financial failure from the start.

Although most shows before the twenties are listed as being produced by the "Messrs." Shubert, it was clearly Lee who was the force behind the company's occasional productions of classics, serious plays, and experimental works. In 1911, for example, Lee would sign Max Reinhardt and his Deutsches Theatre Company for a series of productions at the Casino. The full series never materialized, but Reinhardt did send over his *Sumurun,* an experimental wordless play in nine scenes, which opened in January 1912 and played for two months at the Casino, before touring to Shubert houses in Chicago and Boston.

Lee had also presented George Bernard Shaw's *Widowers' Houses* in 1907, and his *Fanny's First Play* would open at the Comedy Theatre in September 1912 and run for almost eight months. Lee would manage to produce Shaw's translation of Siegfried Trebitsch's *Jitta's Atonement* in 1923, but the Shuberts were never again able to come to terms with the playwright about his own work. In response to a 1913 letter asking to produce *The Philanderer,* Shaw suggested that it was "too late in the season," and the next year he vetoed Lee's request to present *Great Catherine* on the grounds that the play was "too expensive for vaudeville and too short for regular theatre."

In the same year, Shaw entered into negotiations with Lee about an American production of *Pygmalion,* but he insisted that Mrs. Patrick Campbell be hired as the star. Lee, however, found the actress's terms "prohibitive." In 1915, Lee tried once more to obtain rights to several of Shaw's plays, but again he was put off by "the outrageous demands of the stars." The relationship between Shaw and Lee Shubert, it seems clear, was hardly the meeting of true minds, and the wary playwright once remarked to his friend Harley Granville Barker that he was being "Shubertized in small packages."

III
THE TEENS:
BUILDING
AN EMPIRE

The thing I care most about, anyway, is to do
whatever I set out to do. I mean what I say
when I tell you that I don't care much about
the money involved. I don't keep any 'union
hours.' I work night and day.

LEE SHUBERT
In American Magazine,
October 1921

From the outset, the Shuberts, as practical businessmen, had detested the power of the critics to make or break their shows. Their point of view was made clear by Lee when he wrote: "Why should any man, or any dozen men, have the right to render pontifical judgment upon productions costing thousands of dollars and giving employment, first and last, to scores of people? . . . I have presented plays that did not deserve to succeed and have been the first to agree with the critics who said so . . . But I do object to having my property sacrificed to make a smart aleck's holiday, or to feed fat a writer's vanity, or to enable him to settle a grudge."

In an interview, Donald Flamm, who worked for the Shubert press office during the late teens, emphasized the wariness the Shuberts felt toward writers. "During the three years that I worked for Lee," Flamm said, "I don't recall him ever granting a personal interview to any newspaper man. I really think he distrusted the press." Lee and J.J. banned critics left and right after reading unfavorable reviews of their shows. Perhaps their most spectacular casting of a critic into outer darkness had come in March 1915, when they banned Alexander Woollcott of the *Times* from all Shubert theatres as a result of his less than enthusiastic review of a farce called *Taking Chances,* which they had presented at the Thirty-ninth Street Theatre. Woollcott's biographer, Samuel Hopkins Adams, speculated that the Shuberts, as "shrewd analysts of trends . . . may have sensed the *Times'* increasing independence and figured that to discipline the paper and its critic would be a useful lesson to other newspapers which might be tempted to follow a bad example." But if that was the case, they were doomed to disappointment. The *Times* countered with an injunction restraining Lee and J.J. from barring Woollcott and eventually the paper dropped all Shubert advertising. Later the Shuberts managed to win a reversal in the courts, but the loss of advertising space in the *Times* was highly inconvenient and they eventually patched up the matter.

Woollcott was far from being the only critic banned by the Shuberts; in later years a similar fate awaited a number of others, including Percy Hammond, George S. Kaufman, and Walter Winchell. Hammond, of the *Herald Tribune,* was not admitted to the Shuberts' theatres for several years because of invidious comparisons of Winter Garden shows with the *Ziegfeld Follies.* In 1919, when Kaufman was drama editor at the *New York Times,* he panned a Shubert musical called *Hello, Alexander,* which resulted in his being banned from Shubert houses for the rest of his tenure on the newspaper. Winchell would later be rusticated for several years for his unfavorable review of a Shubert-managed 1927 musical, *Lovely Lady.* A desperate Boston critic named George Holland, who was banned from the four Shubert-owned theatres (out of a total of five) in that city had himself appointed a deputy fire inspector on the assumption that he could not be denied entry to any building. He remained resolutely banned.

In the summer of 1909, Lee and J.J. had established their own theatrical newspaper, *The New York Review,* which they would continue to publish until 1931. Like their earlier, more modest publication *The Show, The Review* was fundamentally an extension of the Shubert press department. Strictly speaking, however, it was not a Shubert publication at all—a technicality that Lee would point out on numerous occasions. In fact, the paper was a separate corporation, headed by Dora's husband Milton Wolf, in which Lee and J.J. owned

The Shubert press department. The office shown in the photograph was probably the one located at the rear of the mezzanine in the Forty-fourth Street Theatre during the teens and early twenties. Donald Flamm, who worked there, recalled that the space was cramped and dingy and that "the orchestra music, singing and frequent applause on matinee days were most distracting." The press office was later moved to somewhat less primitive quarters in a brownstone on West Forty-fifth Street, afterwards the site of the Hotel Piccadilly.

The front page of the first issue of the Shuberts' theatrical newspaper, The New York Review, *August 29, 1909. In fact, the Shuberts felt it prudent to disclaim control of the paper. Lee wrote to Charles Daniel, the advertising manager of* The Review, *that in all business correspondence, "I simply want you to say that I am interested in this publication." Yet, Lee and J.J. clearly controlled content; on another occasion, Lee would point out firmly to Daniel that he expected to be consulted about which stars were featured on the paper's front page. "Do not use people like Alice Brady who don't do us a bit of good," he wrote. "Use only people who are working for us." John Shubert claimed that his father and his uncle lost more than a million dollars on the paper over the years.*

a majority of the stock. The editor of *The Review*, Sam Weller, had formerly handled press for the Shuberts, and he visited Lee weekly for stories. Those that related to the Syndicate were carefully checked by Shubert lawyer William Klein. *The Review* consistently lost money, since its actual paid circulation was less than 1,000, and more than 5,000 copies were regularly printed, mostly for free distribution in the theatre district. Yet, the point, of course, was not to make money on *The Review*, but to use it to fill theatre seats.

The paper's editorial policy involved a distinct bias toward Shubert shows, as well as healthy contempt for Actors' Equity, theatre critics, and especially for anyone connected with the Syndicate. In fact, *The Review* was, in a sense, one of the Shuberts' chief tools in the war against Klaw and Erlanger. As one of its reporters, Colgate Baker, wrote, "Lee Shubert's strategy was masterly and practically unbeatable. His main objective was to destroy the Syndicate by taking away all the big producers allied with the Trust." One by one, Baker noted, "the great producing managers deserted the Syndicate and came over to the Shubert camp." But many of them "were afraid of the *Morning Telegraph* and what that venomous Syndicate organ would do to them if they went over to the Shuberts," so *The Review* was created in part "to spike the guns of the Syndicate organ, and to protect producers who fled from the Syndicate to the Shuberts."

The somewhat ham-handed quality of the paper's approach to the Syndicate and its allies is suggested by two headlines from January of 1910, the first of which notes, on the ninth, that "Competition Has Given Authors, Actors, Managers Opportunities They Never Could Have Had Under Monopolistic Conditions—the Young Playwright Now Gets Hearing—The Actor Can Select His Own Part and Name His Own Salary—Both Can Look Managers in the Eye and Tell Them Where To Go." On the thirtieth, *The Review* attacked from another familiar quarter: "Exhibition of Bare Feminine Flesh and Prurient Posturing by the Oriental Rose Is the Lewdest, Most Sordidly Vulgar Ever Seen in a Broadway Playhouse—Theatre Is Under Direct Control of Syndicate 'Chiefs' and the Disgusting Show Could Not Be Given Without Their Sanction." Although Erlanger and his partners had been the source of scurrilous press attacks against all three Shubert brothers since the turn of the century, they were enraged at *The Review*'s blatant anti-Syndicate policy. Yet, there was little they could do about it. Increasingly, the Shuberts were gaining the upper hand in the theatre business—building, buying, and leasing theatres in New York and on the road, producing and touring more and more shows, and recruiting stronger allies in their struggle with the Syndicate.

Basically, Sam's Open Door Policy worked. By the season of 1910–1911, Lee and J.J. controlled some seventy important theatres in large towns around the country, including thirteen in New York City. In addition, in the spring of 1910, about 1200 small-town houses banded together to form the National Theatre Owners Association, which was dedicated to independent booking. All of this gave Lee and J.J. an edge on the Syndicate, which by now was on the verge of dissolving anyway. By 1913, Hayman, Nixon, and Zimmerman had all retired; Frohman would die on the *Lusitania* two years later. In 1918, Klaw and Erlanger quarreled, Klaw departed, and Erlanger became, for all intents and purposes, the Syndicate. By the early twenties the theatre wars would be history—and, as some believed, the Shuberts would have become the Syndicate all over again.

In order to feed their houses across the country, Lee and J.J. had had to be increasingly active as producers, presenting an average of a dozen shows a year on Broadway by the early teens. Many were simply designed to play for a while in New York and then to tour as long as the traffic would bear. But a number of the Broadway shows were major box-office successes. *Bunty Pulls the Strings,* for example, which the Shuberts produced with William A. Brady at the Comedy Theatre in the fall of 1911, was a palpable hit, which played for almost 400 performances. A rather saccharine little comedy about middle-class Scottish life by Graham Moffat, the play has since sunk without a trace. But at the time it was warmly commended by the prestigious *Theatre Magazine* for its "wholesome, homely truth." In May 1912 the magazine reported that *Bunty* had earned the impressive sum of $1,162,000.

George Ingleton and Molly Pearson in Bunty Pulls the Strings, *1911.* Bunty, *a highly successful British import, must have been a great satisfaction to the Shuberts and their co-producer William A. Brady, since it received nearly unanimous rave reviews—a phenomenon with which Lee and J.J. were not overly familiar. Alan Dale, the acid critic of* The American, *was uncharacteristically beside himself with joy. The actors, he wrote, "were all uncriticisable. One could sit there and enjoy their work. And when a critic can do that he is a happy chap. 'Bunty Pulls the Strings' is irresistible from start to finish, and those who miss it will live to kick themselves. And they will deserve it."*

Indeed, as Lee would later tell an *American Magazine* reporter, he and his brother had learned that audiences "will go down in their pockets and pay gladly, if you will give them something that will make them laugh." Or—while he did not say it—something titillating. Lee and J.J. had also learned that sex sold very nicely—although it sometimes presented certain difficulties. A case in point was *The Lure*.

The Lure was a melodrama by the popular playwright George Scarborough, presented by Lee and J.J. at Maxine Elliott's Theatre in the summer of 1913. Scarborough's forgettable play concerned the white slave menace, a subject guaranteed to stimulate ticket sales in the early years of the century, when so-called Red-Light dramas were all the rage. In September, New York's Chief Magistrate McAdoo closed the play on the grounds of "indecency and a tendency to corrupt public morals." Lee was hailed into court, where he cheerfully agreed to present a special performance of *The Lure* for the grand jury. With equal good humor, he had Scarborough rewrite to suit the jurors' objections and promptly reopened the show. As a result of the publicity, the mediocre little play—now made even less interesting than before—managed a four-and-a-half-month run. The lesson was not lost on Lee and J.J., who, time and again, would attempt to generate controversy about their racier shows, realizing full well that it would help to sell second-rate productions, both in New York and on the road.

Another favorite Shubert promotional ploy was the flamboyant publicity stunt, many of which were concocted by the head of their press office in the early years, a Dane with the curious name of A. Toxen Worm. Worm was almost certainly a mixed blessing. Shubert employees often found him eccentric, suspicious, and difficult, with a particularly devastating sense of humor. "You have a nest of fairies, as you well know, in that New York office," he once wrote to J.J., "but instead of touching them with a wand, occasionally, somebody armed with a horsewhip ought to go in there and clean up." His low-comedy ire could even be directed against entire cities. Worm especially disliked Chicago, where he had served two stints, and he noted in his will "the earnest hope that God may take care of Chicago in the future, so as to enable it to live down its miserable past and wretched present."

Worm engineered hundreds of publicity stunts, frequently in dubious, even bizarre taste. In 1912, for example, when white pigeons were hard to obtain for the Gertrude Hoffmann show *Broadway to Paris,* Worm suggested that there be a press release noting "that this particular market is cornered by the Chinese, who buy these birds to accompany the flight . . . of their souls into kingdom come. However, the difficulty of getting these birds will make a good story for the reason named, and I shall also advertise for the pigeons at liberty and not employed presently in Chinese funerals."

When Sarah Bernhardt's leg was amputated in 1915, Worm suggested that she be signed for a "Real Farewell Tour or Post Amputation Tour." "There is no question in my mind," he wrote, "that Bernhardt's engagement will be a great success; first, because of the news interest attached to seeing a woman of her age and her standing appearing with a cork leg. The newspapers will eat this up, with

The Agent on his Star

Caricature of the head of the Shubert press office during the teens, A. Toxen Worm, and Lee Shubert. Donald Flamm, who worked for Worm, described him as a "stout Yul Brynner who sort of waddled when he walked and seemed grumpy even when he liked you." Yet, Flamm noted, "he was recognized as tops in his profession as a theatrical public relations expert." Although J.J. complained in 1912 about Worm's "dictatorial attitude," five years later he would describe their press chief in a telegram to Lee as "forceful" and "someone who can preach the Shubert doctrine better than anyone else."

Photograph of the Shubert star Gaby Deslys in 1907; and a Gaby souvenir pincushion in the shape of a slipper, sold to mark her seventy-fifth performance at the Winter Garden in December of 1911. Gaby was furiously publicized by Shubert press director, A. Toxen Worm. A 1911 letter from the manager of a Chicago theatre where she was to appear remarked that "it is the ultra-sensational A. Toxen Worm stuff which will bring in the money. For instance we could make much out of the carrying about of her pearls—have the police appoint special detectives just to guard them. If necessary we might even have a false robbery."

descriptions of her legs, how it feels to play on a cork leg, etc., because it is something that no other woman did before." He added as a kind of genteel afterthought, that the Shuberts ought to tour her, "because she will be regarded as the impersonation of the undaunted spirit of France, and you know how much sympathy there is for France in this country now."

Some of Worm's most effective stunts were for Gaby Deslys, the French singer, dancer and pantomimist, who worked for the Shuberts from 1911 to 1914 in such shows as *Belle of Bond Street* and *Honeymoon Express*. Among his efforts on her behalf, Worm arranged stories linking Deslys to the recently disposed King Manuel of Portugal. He invented a passenger on the boat that brought Deslys to America who fell so madly in love with her that he had the ship's baker imprint her name on the rolls he ate for breakfast each morning. And he arranged for the star to dine with a baby elephant on the stage of the Hippodrome.

His efforts on Deslys's behalf were so outrageous, in fact, that even J.J. began to become anxious about them. But Worm assured him that "once the ball of this sort has been started rolling on its way, you cannot stop it in the middle of its flight. Mr. Jolson . . . and others are jealous because of the publicity which Gaby is getting, and they are trying to put the brakes on." Worm reasoned, however, that if "Gaby were not sensational, you wouldn't be paying her the salary that you are paying her."

Touring formed an important part of Lee and J.J.'s business at this point in their careers, although a notably risky one. In the season of 1910–1911, for example, they sent out three companies of their pres-

The Grand Opera House, Wilkes-Barre, Pennsylvania, 1912, an early Shubert road house. The poster advertises a pre-Broadway tryout of an ill-fated operetta, The Love School, *which was produced by the Shuberts. The local newspaper noted that "the blue pencil will have to be used freely" if the show was to receive a New York City production. In fact,* The Love School, *like dozens of other Shubert shows, appears to have died on the road.*

tigious 1909 Broadway success, Clyde Fitch's *The City*, a relatively sophisticated melodrama about the evil influence of urban life on a family coming to the city from a small town. The play, by one of the country's most celebrated authors, had had an excellent run of six months in New York, and the Shuberts had every reason to believe that the show would do well on the road.

The City was notable as one of the first Broadway plays to contain profanity. During the second act a dope fiend exclaimed, "You're a God damn liar," and then shot his wife, who, it turned out, was also his half-sister. Several audience members fainted on opening night in New York, an event which proved so newsworthy that the show's road manager tried to hire fainters for every opening around the country. But small-town America was not much interested. As Fred Kimball, manager of one of the companies, noted in a November 1910 letter, "the universal opinion is that it is a brilliantly acted play, the story horrible in the extreme, which attracts the curious. The story keeps the young and timid away. It is essentially a New York and Chicago attraction." J.J. ruefully responded that he had "thought the *The City* would make a big hit all over the country, but . . . the

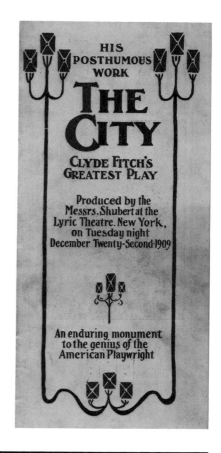

HIS POSTHUMOUS WORK

THE CITY

CLYDE FITCH'S GREATEST PLAY

Produced by the Messrs. Shubert at the Lyric Theatre, New York, on Tuesday night December Twenty-Second 1909

An enduring monument to the genius of the American Playwright

Program cover for Clyde Fitch's The City *(1909), and a photograph of a scene from the play, with Walter Hampden and Tully Marshal. It is not unlikely that the Shuberts' connection with Fitch came through their mutual friend and business partner Richard Mansfield. Whatever the case, Fitch was one of the few distinguished American playwrights to be produced by the Shuberts. The fact that* The City, *a rather grim melodrama, did badly on the road only helped to strengthen J.J.'s conviction that the future of the theatre business lay with popular plays. Lee may have agreed in principle, but he never entirely ceased to be attracted to more serious work. That many of the serious plays lost money was one of chief sources of tension between the two men.*

public doesn't seem to want it. I think I will turn Christian Scientist and sit back and hold my thumbs."

From the beginning the Shuberts had kept constant pressure on road managers to report in detail and to keep expenses down. Guido Marburg, manager of *The Witching Hour* company, reported early in the century that an understudy who was "a regular scandal monger," as well as "a useless expense and a polite nuisance," had been fired when the tour was losing money. She had threatened to sue the company. Meanwhile, a company carpenter had been overcharging the show for tacks to the tune of a dollar a week, as well as selling free passes. The stagehands were irate because they had been laid off for Holy Week in Detroit at a saving of a hundred dollars, "as, in my opinion, the production needed no repairs." Marburg notes that the stagehands "spoke insultingly of the Shuberts." Another carpenter, however, may have been in a cheerier frame of mind since he "got drunk on tour, which I condoned." But a third carpenter, working for the touring company of *The Revellers,* Marburg pointed out, "was caught 'red-handed' by me, in an endeavor to trail his wife, at your expense to Washington. Further a neat little 'graft' was arranged by him to have you pay $5—every time a car was loaded or unloaded."

The theme of cutting costs runs through all the Shubert correspondence for half a century. A manager named Stanley Sharpe wrote to J.J. from Chicago in 1902, for example, noting that "I got away with the amounts you told me to pay show girls and dancers also boys: Show Girls $20—Dancers:20, Boys—18–20—I had a lot of kicks but told them if they didn't like it they knew what they could do so have not heard anything more—." Sharpe casually adds a personal note: "I did not charge my salary last week not knowing what it was as you did not tell me before you left Chicago."

From the early teens onward, much of the Shuberts' road activity was managed by E. R. "Ma" Simmons. Simmons was a dance director, casting director, and general assistant to J.J., specializing in the production details involved with musicals and revues. From 1912, for some forty years, until he retired in his mid-eighties, Simmons was the consummate Broadway character. Known as "Ma" because of his effeminacy, he was famous for riding through Times Square in an open car with one of his various pets on the seat next to him, among

Photograph of E. R. "Ma" Simmons ("when he was young"), inscribed to his employer J.J. Shubert. The Shuberts' wry and eccentric casting and dance director was also costume supervisor for road shows. A road company actor once wrote to Simmons, complaining that his costume was rapidly decaying. "I think if your second act clothes are disintegrating completely," Simmons responded, "it might help the sale of tickets. The only thing is, if you appeared without clothes in the second act, somebody might be killed in the rush."

them a police dog, a cheetah, and a lion named Thomas, which he was finally forced to retire to a zoo in the thirties because of complaints from other residents of his apartment house.

In his autobiography, *Much Ado About Me,* Fred Allen recalled Simmons as the keeper of the Shubert wardrobe department. "Ma's memory," he said, "was uncanny. In August, when the new Shubert shows were in rehearsal and the older shows were being readied to go on the road, Ma might be supplying wardrobes for eight or ten different shows" from the Shuberts' "massive wardrobe limbo." Allen marveled that "Ma knew the name of every chorus girl who had torn her farthingale at *The Passing Show* rehearsal in New York, the name of *The Blossom Time* principal whose peruke was too tight, and how many buttons were off the chorus boys' trousers in the road company in Chicago."

Simmons was also in charge of what Allen called "another old Shubert custom—cutting the cast . . . A Shubert musical show always opened in New York with a top cast. If a show was a smash hit, after it had been running for a few weeks some of the minor principals were replaced with cheaper actors. When the show finished its New York run and left for the road, high-salaried principals who could be spared were replaced, scenes were eliminated, and occasionally the chorus was cut down. Names were needed in Chicago itself, but when that run was finished and the show started on split weeks and one-nighters around the Midwest, chorus boys and girls replaced dancing and singing principals in the sketches. After these dates, a Shubert musical leaving for California was cut down again until only one or two of the stars remained . . . ."

Beginning in 1911, the Shuberts established a long-standing connection with the Yiddish theatre star Bertha Kalich. In February of that year they began to tour an English-language version of Kalich's great success, *The Kreutzer Sonata*, which had been written for her by the famous playwright Jacob Gordin. Touring a Yiddish play, even

Photograph of Bertha Kalich, the Yiddish theatre star who frequently toured for the Shuberts. The historian of Yiddish theatre, David Lifson, has pointed out that Kalich "was the first of the Yiddish actors to go to the English-speaking stage. [The earlier historian] Gorin prophesied that 'her leaving the Yiddish theatre . . . was a portent of what would happen to the best strength of the Yiddish theatre which will be stolen away by the power of the American dollar.' Goren's prophecy became a reality through the years."

in translation, was risky. Shubert press representatives urged Lee and J.J. to "keep her out of small towns," to "play in larger cities where there are more Jews," and to "cut out Yiddish poster advertising since it makes Madame look like she's doing a play in a foreign language." But reviews of the play, about a woman's need for fulfillment as a human being, were highly enthusiastic, the show made money, and Kalich would continue to be associated with Lee and J.J. until the mid-twenties, frequently going on the road in revivals of Gordin's play.

Touring in this period was a difficult proposition for everyone involved. Kalich, for example, complained that the wrong scenery had arrived for her opening at Troy, New York. William Moxon, road manager for *The City,* wrote about his troubles with a Miss Lowry, a disruptive actress, and Kimball, the manager of another road company of the show, complained about an actor with a drinking problem. As if that were not enough, J.J. wrote to Kimball, cautioning him to keep his expenses down. "Every time we save $2," J.J. informed him, "we save $100 as we have 50 shows." There were storms, floods, and accidents, among them a bizarre mishap in 1910 on the Shuberts' tour of Anna Pavlova and Mikail Mordkin in Canada, during which "a sword which Mordkin waved over his head broke and flew into the audience embedding itself into the skull of one of the spectators sitting in the eighth row."

Myrtle Edwards Comstock, an advance agent who traveled ahead of shows on the road, handling publicity and advertising, had some special problems. In 1913, she would write from Chicago, where she was promoting *The Red Petticoat,* to report the hostility of male managers. "I have not started anything, but I can finish strong and they will find it out to their sorrow if they don't leave me alone . . . It is at bottom a question of sex. They will not have a woman if they can help it. I think every woman in your employ can tell you the same."

Eddie Cantor would later write irately that chorus girls in his touring show "didn't stay sober enough to do their jobs." Al Jolson, who detested touring, wrote to J.J. from the road in 1917 that "I have played thirty one-nighters in succession and I don't think I can stand it much longer. The food is terrible, the hotels worse; I have had one

Max Rabinoff and G. P. Centanini

ANNOUNCE THE FIRST AMERICAN TOUR OF

Mlle. Anna Pavlowa
M. Mikail Mordkin

—— AND ——

The Imperial Russian Ballet

With Complete Orchestra.   Theodore Stier, Conductor

By Special Arrangement with the Russian Government
and Metropolitan Opera Company, New York

Bureau of Publicity, 145 West 45th Street, New York
BEN H. ATWELL   -   -   -   Director

Letterhead of the 1910–11 Pavlova-Mordkin North American tour, handled by the Shuberts. For the most part, Lee and J.J. did not tour dance or concert events. The Pavlova-Mordkin tour was undoubtedly their response to the developing American interest in the Russian ballet at the time. Their enthusiasm for the dance was probably dampened considerably, however, by a curious accident in Hamilton, Ontario, in which an audience member was seriously wounded by a broken sword, wielded by Mordkin. Mordkin was threatened with arrest unless a $5000 bond was posted, and the ultimate result for Lee and J.J. was a protracted and costly lawsuit.

good meal this month. If I don't get a good meal pretty soon, you can use me for a xylophone. I doubt if I can hold out unless you send me something to eat by parcel post."

By 1913, problems had begun to develop with the road, in no small part because of the constant warfare between the Shuberts and the Syndicate. Attendance was declining as the quality and quantity of productions emanating from New York fell off and as motion pictures became an increasingly popular entertainment medium. By the mid-teens, it appeared that the road might shortly die altogether. The Shuberts—or Lee, at any rate—now saw the need to diversify by joining the new motion picture industry that was threatening their world.

"The motion pictures have hurt the Hippodrome in two ways," the

Shuberts noted in a press release when they dropped their lease on the theatre in 1915. "In the first place the people who thronged the huge galleries stopped coming to the Hippodrome, and instead went to the numerous neighborhood [movie] theatres around the places where they lived. Secondly, all the thrills which used to be characteristic of the Hippodrome productions have been copied, introduced, and improved upon by the motion picture people, and whereas the Hippodrome used to score a sensation by showing a thousand or more people on the stage, it is possible now to see two or three thousand people in a moving picture, for the expenditure of a nickel or a dime." The assessment of the problem was quite accurate, and the Shuberts characteristically unloaded the house and began their own foray into motion picture production, creating a Shubert film studio.

Although the Shuberts were first and foremost theatre owners and theatrical producers, over the years they would continually diversify, becoming involved in several other potentially profitable areas of business. Lee and J.J., for example, were major owners of non-theatrical real estate, including a number of shops, office buildings, and hotels in New York, Boston, and Chicago. Within the entertainment business, the brothers would have two basically unproductive forays into vaudeville and a rather extended and painful excursion into the motion picture industry.

As early as 1908 the Shuberts were permitting Adolph Zukor and Marcus Loewe to show their films in several Shubert theatres on Sundays. Lee and J.J. later became partners with Loewe in a motion picture theatre chain, and eventually started a company to book feature films around the country. In 1914 they entered the film business as producers, with a studio in Fort Lee, New Jersey, then the center of film making in America. The idea was to produce films of Shubert plays at a new studio, Peerless, to be built in Fort Lee. Their partner in the studio was Jules Brulatour, a French film maker who had previously financed some pictures made by Shubert ally William Brady.

Brulatour, Lee later wrote, was "polished, suave and resourceful," and "had a way with him that carried conviction. A smooth talker, he could carry his point almost before the man with whom he was dealing realized it." E.F. Albee, the vaudeville magnate, who had had dealings with him, warned Lee: "'Look out for that man! He's the shrewdest article you ever did business with. He'll get your eye teeth if you don't watch your step.'" Meanwhile, Lewis J. Selznick had convinced Lee to invest in his new World Film Corporation. The result was the Shubert Feature Film Corporation, which produced motion pictures for World at the Peerless studio. In 1915 the three entities were consolidated as World Film.

The connections between Broadway and World were always close. Over the years, World filmed a number of Shubert stage shows, including *The City, Old Dutch, Trilby,* and *America.* Shubert associates also supplied material for pictures. Brady's *The Gentleman from Mississippi, The Whip,* and *The Pit* were filmed by the studio, as were several Owen Davis plays, among them *The Family Cupboard* (which had been produced by Brady), *The Marked Woman,* and *The Wishing Ring,* a classic picture directed by a talented Frenchman, Maurice Tourneur.

Initially, World was a great success, producing first-rate pictures with such theatrical luminaries as Lillian Russell, Wilton Lackaye, Lew Fields, Holbrook Blinn, Lionel Barrymore, and Brady's daughter, the popular actress Alice Brady. Soon an allied studio, Paragon, was built next door to Peerless, with Maurice Tourneur in charge. World was now producing a considerable number of films of high quality. But there were financial problems which resulted in Brulatour and Selznick leaving the company. Selznick took with him one of World's most popular stars, actress Clara Kimball Young.

In 1916, Brady, a longtime Shubert associate, took over as director general with considerable fanfare. An advertisement in the May issue of the *Saturday Evening Post* featured dignified portraits of Lee and Brady and a dozen of their stars. Brady solemnly addressed theatre-goers about the new challenge that awaited him. "From now on," the text by his picture notes, "I supervise PERSONALLY every World Picture Play from start to finish. Please do not think I am lending my name—I am giving myself. I bring to motion pictures the experiences I acquired in the past twenty-five years in the dramatic world." From across the page Lee nods enthusiastic agreement, as he informs motion picture exhibitors that Brady "brings to the screen all of his high ideals, all of his ability as a director and all his ambition to win the

Lobby card for The Hand Invisible *(1919) with Montagu Love, produced by the Shuberts' World Film Corporation. Film historian Kevin Lewis has suggested that "what doomed World was its lack of real film stars and poor choice of material. An inordinate amount of the films released by the studio starred the same people—June Elvidge, Montagu Love, Kitty Gordon, Carlyle Blackwell, Arthur Ashley—in the same stories." Montagu Love, for example, was perennially cast as "the hardened ex-convict or ruthless industrialist type," and too many of the World films were "thrill-a-minute melodramas without any distinction."*

friendship of a larger audience. . . . World Pictures, from this time on, will occupy a place of their own."

In fact, Brady could not save World Film. The studio was overproducing and the quality of the films began to drop disastrously. Production was cut in half, but for the most part the work did not improve significantly. In 1916 and 1917, most of the French directors and technicians whom Brulator had hired left to follow Selznick or to

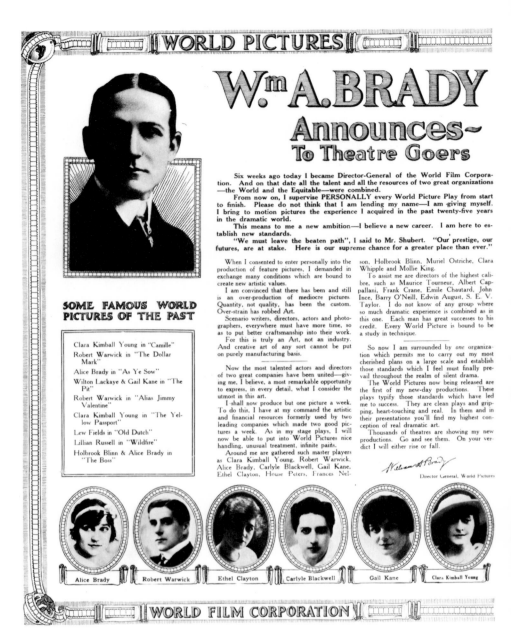

Advertisement announcing the reorganization of the Shuberts' World Film Corporation in 1916. When Brady took over as general manager of World, the company was in a period of decline. Within two years, he had given up hope for the studio and taken another job, pointing out to Moving Picture World *in February of 1918 that "I have resigned a position paying $100,000 a*

year because as conditions are I don't feel I can earn it. You know if a stage producer puts on a play and he feels that it is not going to be a success at first he can explain the situation to his players and obtain a temporary concession in the way of salaries. . . . Conditions mean nothing to motion picture players."

take jobs at other studios. Brady resigned as general manager in 1918, although he continued on the company's board of directors. Lee, who was a director and vice-president, resigned in December 1918, and almost immediately joined the board of directors of Goldwyn Pictures. The last films produced by World were released in 1919.

The Shuberts continued to own the Peerless property, but it was of no particular importance after 1919 as the film industry increasingly became centered in California. A few Yiddish films were made at the studio during the thirties, and from time to time Brady employed it as a rehearsal hall for his productions, among them his famous *Street Scene* of 1929. In later years Lee and J.J. used the structure as a scenery and property warehouse. It burned to the ground in 1958, taking with it the scenery for many of the classic Shubert shows, and probably the only copies of many World films as well. Of the more than 350 films made by the Shuberts at World, only a handful survive.

A major part of the Shuberts' prosperity during the teens would come from their Broadway musicals, which both brothers produced, although they became J.J.'s specialty. Musical revues, J.J. found, were particularly cheap and easy to mount since little in the way of a script was necessary and existing acts, songs, scenery, and costumes could be plugged into a revue or removed at will. Ziegfeld, the Shuberts' prime competitor in the revue field, spent endless energy and immense sums of money on his products; J.J., on the other hand, developed a kind of assembly-line technique which allowed him to produce a standardized revue. Legitimate shows were not allowed to play on Sundays in New York until 1940, but "concerts" were permitted, and J.J. took full advantage of the opportunities they presented by offering Sunday night vaudeville at his Winter Garden Theatre. "After a half-dozen Sunday concerts," John Shubert noted, "J.J. would have acquired enough new audience-tested material to build his next revue around." The "only difference between Father's products," he once noted, "was their titles."

What distinguished the Ziegfeld revue from its Shubert counterpart, according to John, "can best be summed up by the fact that Ziegfeld took his time to perfect every phase of his production, and the Shuberts did not. My father, always under pressure from his brother or his bookers to get out an attraction before it was even ready to be seen, just to fill theatrical playing time on the road and in New York, was unable to devote his full personal supervision and thought to his projects, and consequently he never achieved the perfection he undoubtedly wanted."

The venue for many of J.J.'s musicals and revues was the Winter Garden Theatre, built far uptown on Broadway at Fiftieth Street. The theatre, which was opened in 1911, was unusual for Broadway because it had been remodeled from an existing building, Alfred Gwynne Vanderbuilt's American Horse Exchange. The result of the remodeling was a handsome 1600-seat house, although an extremely wide one because it followed the original lines of the Horse Exchange. As remodeled by architect William A. Swasey, the new theatre included an auditorium decorated in a garden motif, complete with trellised walls and ceiling, a promenade at the rear of the auditorium, and a cabaret called the Palais de Danse.

Lee says that he was warned by old Broadway hands that the site was too far above Times Square: "'You will be in the woods up there. The public will never find you. You might as well be in Harlem. Your shows will starve to death.'" And indeed, as Lee noted, the theatre site was then far out of the way for theatre-goers. "At that time Broadway above 45th Street was absolutely dead at night except for the customary saloon at almost every corner. Opposite the Horse Exchange was a barroom of the old style, and adjoining it was a blacksmith shop where horses were shod almost on the Broadway sidewalk all day long." The Winter Garden's other near neighbors included a carriage factory and the trolley car sheds of the New York Street Railway Company. Yet audiences were to come in droves to this apparently unpromising neighborhood.

The Winter Garden opened in March of 1911 with a curtain-raiser called *Bow Sing* (a one-act "Chinese" opera) and *La Belle Paree*, yet another of the revue-*cum*-vaudeville shows so popular at the time. The show contained a somewhat lackluster score by Frank Tours, with interpolations by Jerome Kern, and it featured a now forgotten performer named Mitzi Hajos, whose musical revues were later to become a staple of Shubert touring.

Basically, *La Belle Paree* was a girlie show of the sort that was soon

Winter Garden and Broadway, New York City.

Postcard view of Broadway, looking north, showing the Winter Garden Theatre, 1916; and a photograph, about 1910, with an artist's mock-up of proposed changes to be made to the exterior of the American Horse Exchange at the time of its remodeling as the Winter Garden. In fact, as the 1916 photograph indicates, the changes to the façade of the Horse Exchange were far more extensive than had originally been planned, especially to the south wing of the building at Broadway and Fiftieth Street. The second and third floors in the south wing housed Lee and J.J.'s cabaret, the Palais de Danse.

to be the Winter Garden's trademark. The theatre, as a flyer for a later show noted, was renowned for its "far-famed New York Winter Garden Beauty Brigade of Bewitching Broadway Blondes and Brunettes." The opportunities which such shows offered the theatre's chorus girls were well known. One of them, Marion Mooney, who first appeared in *La Belle Paree,* suggested that "the average Winter

Garden life of a girl is five years. During that period she marries and retires altogether or she becomes a principal in the Winter Garden or some production." Half of those who marry, Mooney suggested, "marry men they met while playing at the Winter Garden. All of them receive notes from men who have seen them from the orchestra seats. These they ignore but eventually the man, if he is at all serious, manages to find some mutual friend to introduce him."

Potential suitors had plenty to look at onstage. The early Winter Garden shows, in fact, were thought by many to be unusually graphic in their advertisement of chorus girl charms. A 1912 show, *Broadway to Paris,* for example, led a critic into a meditation on stage nudity. "As for their dress," he wrote, "their un-dress, their garb and their un-garb—well, one got used to it after the first hour. Some of the little dears wore on their legs—that is, limbs—what those limbs were born in. Others wore tights and fleshings, and it is wonderful how much more dressed a gell looks in tights than in an un-tighted leg." A Los Angeles detective, who arrested a number of *Broadway to Paris* cast members in the touring company for "participating in an indecent production," was somewhat less broad-minded. "It's the rawest show I've ever seen on the stage," he reported, "and I've seen plenty of raw shows."

Interior of the restaurant floor of Lee and J.J.'s "'Palais de Danse' Restaurant and Persian Ball Room, Adjoining the Winter Garden," about 1912. In a 1913 draft application to extend the cabaret's closing hour beyond one o'clock, a Shubert employee, Stanley Sharpe, explained its mission to the "most prominent stars of the theatrical profession." His letter points out that it is "frequently midnight before they are ready to leave their dressing rooms and the time from then till one o'clock is all too brief for them to enjoy what is really the only recreation they get. They meet and commingle at the Palais de Danse each evening and I petition that the closing hour be extended."

La Belle Paree included one performer who was to be of immense importance to the Shuberts in years to come—a former minstrel man named Al Jolson, who presented a rather outré blackface number called "Paris Is a Paradise for Coons." Born Asa Yoelson, the son of a Russian cantor, Jolson got his start in burlesque. By the end of the first decade of the century, he had become the star of Dockstader's

Minstrels, surpassing in popularity even the legendary Lew Dockstader himself. Early in his career it became apparent that Jolson had immense power over audiences—a kind of rare personal magnetism that led critic O.O. McIntyre to compare him to such stars as Mansfield and Duse. He also possessed an ego to match his talent, which equipped him to negotiate toe to toe with J.J. Shubert and often to emerge the winner.

J.J. fulminated about Jolson's self-serving approach to show business, but there was little he could do about it if he wanted to keep his discovery under Shubert management. In 1911, as well as performing in ten shows a week at the Winter Garden, Jolson was "singing in

A scene from La Belle Paree, *1911, the opening production at the Winter Garden, and the show in which Al Jolson made his Broadway debut. The show's opening drew lukewarm reviews, although Jolson's songs and blackface comedy turns were generally well received by the press. By the third night of the run Jolson had hit his stride and was well on his way to becoming a sensation with Broadway audiences. Characteristically, he left the show claiming illness a week before it was to close; equally characteristically, Lee and J.J. forced him to tour in* La Belle Paree *by threatening to shift all their promotional efforts to his brother Harry, a vaudevillian under contract to them in a show called* The Revue of Revues. *Once Jolson capitulated, Harry claimed he was forced out of his own show.*

phonographs and at private recitals three or four times a week." Logically enough, the star developed—or claimed to develop—throat problems and cut several songs from his show. During Christmas week, J.J. wrote to Lee that, "As I expected, it has happened. Mr. Jolson has been giving the worst performances. . . . with a big house tonight the show went rotten." J.J. became more and more wary, complaining to Lee that "this feller Jolson is getting to be a tough proposition. He did not sing any songs yesterday afternoon at all and stayed off in the finale. He does pretty much as he pleases the moment no one is there."

But there were important compensations. From the opening of the Winter Garden through the late teens, Jolson made millions for the Shuberts—and for himself as well—in such shows as *Vera Violetta* (1911), *The Whirl of Society* (1912), *The Honeymoon Express* (1913),

A Winter Garden program cover, 1913, with a chorus girl in a Pierrot costume. The chorus girl became a kind of symbol of the Winter Garden and its shows. As John Shubert would write, "Florenz Ziegfeld had no monopoly on the idea of featuring attractive, well-dressed women on the stages of New York theatres. The Shuberts, too, knew the dollars-and-cents value of chicly attired stars and chorines."

J.J. Shubert and Al Jolson, date unknown. The display of amity does not fully catch the relationship between the two, both of whom possessed larger-than-life-size egos and a certain wariness about the motives of the other. They warred constantly about Jolson's tendency to go AWOL. When it was rumored that Jolson was about to claim illness in order to pursue a lucrative vaudeville tour, J.J. blandly—if somewhat pointedly—noted that "you can put it over on me any time you like, by making believe you are ill." Jolson wrote to J.J. during the tour of Sinbad *in 1921: "My blood is on your hands if this is your way of showing me a good time. Come here yourself. But I am game. I will stick unless the food runs out. Yours in pain—Al."*

Dancing Around (1914), *Robinson Crusoe, Jr.* (1916), and *Sinbad* (1918). For the most part, the Winter Garden shows were loosely plotted star vehicles, in which Jolson, in blackface, played a comic waiter or chauffeur or butler, in several cases opposite Gaby Deslys, the celebrated French entertainer. But Jolson was always the real star, and the shows were invariably designed to permit him a lengthy—and often irrelevant—solo to dazzle the Winter Garden audience. *Sinbad,* for example, which opened in February of 1918, was a Winter Garden formula show, with a banal script by Harold Atteridge that moved Jolson and Company from the "North Shore Country Club" to various parts of the "Perfumed East." Sigmund Romberg's music was as unremarkable as Atteridge's script, but Jolson's performance of such interpolated songs as "Rock-a-bye Your Baby with a Dixie Melody" and "My Mammy" (which he sang on one knee on the famous Winter Garden runway) created a minor sensation. And in spite of lukewarm reviews for everything connected with the show ex-

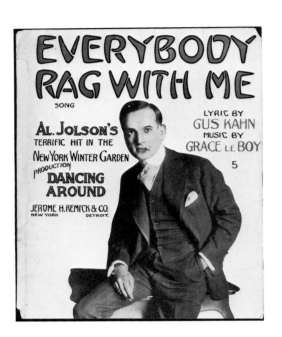

PRETTY PIRATES

Glittering Galaxies of Gorgeous, Glorious, Gladsome Girlies Mirthfully Monopolizing the Mad, Merry hours and the Ten Tremendous Tumultuous scenes of "ROBINSON CRUSOE, Jr."

COURT THEATRE
WHEELING
Thursday, Oct. 18th

CRUSOE GIRLS

A Small Section of the far-famed N. Y. Winter Garden Beauty Brigade of Bewitching Broadway Blondes and Brunettes, who hold Regal Revel in CRUSOE'S Roisterous Rarebit Romp!

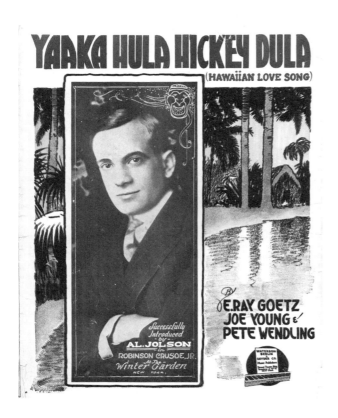

Materials related to Jolson's Shubert shows: (facing page) sheet music cover for "Everybody Rag with Me," Jolson's hit from Dancing Around *(1914); advertising flyer for* Robinson Crusoe, Jr. *(1916); Anna Wheaton and Donald MacDonald in* Honeymoon Express *(1913); (above) sheet music cover for "Yaaka Hula Hickey Dula," from* Robinson Crusoe, Jr.; *sketch by Alois Bohnen for a pirate costume,* Robinson Crusoe, Jr.; *(right) sheet music cover for "Bagdad," from* Sinbad *(1918). Jolson's biographer Herbert Goldman tells of a contemporary view of him as a performer: "'The moment Jolson walked on a stage,' wrote John Crosby, 'you got the impression that something important was going to happen. Frequently, nothing important did happen, but you kept feeling that, in a minute or two, it would.'"*

cept Jolson, *Sinbad* managed a healthy twenty-week run and toured extensively.

Over the years, J.J. alternated threats and flattery to keep Jolson more or less in line. The singer was passionately fond of gambling, and J.J. remonstrated with him about "your association with a lot of race track touts." They were, he wrote, "not what Mr. Al Jolson should be coupled with. You don't know it, but you are a bigger man than you realize and people have a great deal of respect for you." And a better actor than Eddie Cantor, J.J. was quick to point out later, in the wake of *The Jazz Singer*—"not that you haven't always been a better entertainer because Joly is Joly." Jolson no doubt agreed and took out an advertisement in *Variety,* pledging to return to Shubert management after his first film. "You know, baby," he wrote to Lee, enclosing a copy of the ad, "that I wouldn't leave you for all the rest of the managers in the country." At least not for the moment—but the time was coming when Jolson would feel the need to revise his plans.

Jolson's ace in the hole with the Shuberts during the teens and the twenties had been the fact that they were never absolutely sure what their star would do. J.J. wrote nervously—and tellingly—to him in

Photograph of the sometime Shubert star Georgie Price. Price had been a vaudeville entertainer since the early teens, becoming well known in Gus Edwards's extremely popular "school-room" act "Kid Kabaret." By the end of the teens, the Shuberts saw Price, whose fortunes were rising in vaudeville, as a possible replacement for one or the other of their major stars, Eddie Cantor and Al Jolson, should either of them defect. But things worked out badly for Price. As in the case of Jolson's brother Harry, it was widely felt in the theatre world that Lee and J.J. had used Price unfairly, eventually forcing him out of their shows when they no longer needed him. Correspondence from the early twenties between Price and Lee and J.J. suggests that this was precisely what took place.

1917 that "I know you are going to stay with us and I do not want to treat you as an actor, I want to treat you more and more like a friend than anything else." Yet J.J., being no fool, had long been looking for his own ace in the hole—a star who could replace Jolson if necessary. One of the potential replacements was a vaudeville performer named Georgie Price, who was hired in the early twenties when it appeared that both Jolson and their only other star at the time, Eddie Cantor, might decamp.

J.J. clearly treated Price more like an actor than a friend, especially when neither of the stars left once Price had been signed to a long-term contract. Basically, it appears that the Shuberts froze Price out through appalling working conditions and complex and protracted salary disputes. In 1922, for example, Price wrote from the road that "I arrived here this morning, had to deliver my own trunk to the theatre, not an inch of billing, publicity or press matter, not even a dressing room." Eight months later, in Seattle, Price found himself stranded. "If there was no place to work me and it was a case of asking pay without working," he wrote, "I would let it go. But in this instance, I am told to lay off three thousand miles from home, where my expenses go on just the same, while the company plays, and my guarantee has another week to go." J.J. responded to this, Price's fourth communication on the subject, with the request that his fallen star try to "show a little of the milk of human kindness."

It was at the Winter Garden, in 1912, that J.J. had introduced *The Passing Show,* which was to become a feature of the Shubert season for more than a decade. This light summer entertainment borrowed its name from an 1894 hit revue, produced by George Lederer at the Casino. Its basic format was suggested by Ziegfeld's *Follies,* which had been a thorn in J.J.'s side since its highly successful first appearance in 1907, although *The Passing Show,* unlike the *Follies,* tended to feature traditional burlesques of current Broadway successes. The 1912 edition began with "The Ballet of 1830," a rather arch one-act dance piece imported from England, which dealt with love among the nineteenth-century bohemians of Paris. The show's second half was a collection of fairly conventional burlesques of such popular plays of the day as George Broadhurst's *Bought and Paid For* and the

Mollie King and her brother Charles in The Passing Show of 1913. *Burlesques of popular plays from the past season were a convention of the Broadway revue of this period. Here Mollie King satirizes Laurette Taylor as the title character in the popular* Peg o' My Heart; *Charles King impersonates George M. Cohan as Jackson Jones in Cohan's* Broadway Jones. *Among the other recent shows burlesqued were two now forgotten musicals, the extremely successful* Oh! Oh! Delphine, *by the team of C. M. S. McLellan and Ivan Caryll, and* The Sunshine Girl, *which featured Vernon and Irene Castle and was an important influence on the so-called Dance Craze of the teens. Also satirized was* Within the Law, *an example of another fad of the period, the crime-detection melodrama.*

David Belasco success *The Return of Peter Grimm*. The musical numbers were staged by the talented choreographer Ned Wayburn. Among the featured performers were vaudevillian Trixie Friganza and the comedy team of Willie and Eugene Howard, who were later to work in many Shubert productions. J.J. was to present editions of *The Passing Show* more or less yearly throughout the teens and twenties as long as Ziegfeld continued to offer the public his more famous—and more impressive—*Follies*.

J.J. fancied himself a director. Over the years he managed to direct several productions, on his own or with others, and to "supervise" countless musicals and revues, much to the spiritual discomfort of the cast and crew members. Fred Allen recalled J.J.'s director-manqué relationship to the *Passing Show of 1922*, in which he appeared. J.J., he said, was a "small ball of a man. With his short neck and pudgy body he looked like a turtle who had somehow got out of its shell and was standing upright and walking around." At rehearsals, which were held at the Century Theatre, "J.J. sat in a little human tuft, looking more like a turtle than ever as he blinked and gave the impression that his mind was miles away under a lily pad somewhere, and that he wished he were there with it. J.J. rarely smiled. When he did, it was considered a bad omen. Comedians who worked for the Shuberts swore that any comedy lines or funny business that J.J. laughed at during rehearsal were invariably taken out after the show had opened. To a joke, J.J.'s laugh was the kiss of death."

Luckily for Allen, J.J. remained mute and Allen's material stayed in the show, which opened in tryouts at the Apollo in Atlantic City. But there his luck ran out. There was no time for a dress rehearsal, and the director suggested to J.J. that they cancel the opening performance to rehearse. "With the theatre sold out," Allen wrote, "suggesting to J.J. that he return the money was like hinting to a small boy that he give you his ice-cream cone as he is raising it to his mouth to take the first bite. J.J. decided that the show would open, on schedule, and without a dress rehearsal." The curtain finally came down at 3:30 in

Fred Allen, a veteran Shubert comedian, in Lee Shubert's Vogues of 1924, *a revue with the violin-playing French chanteuse Odette Myrtil and comic Jimmy Savo. In his autobiography Allen recalled that "*Vogues *was not a smash hit. Nobody knew why. Alibis ran the gamut: Odette Myrtil was not known to the New York audiences; the people who came to see* Vogues *didn't like it as well as the critics; the show wasn't dirty enough, and so on . . . [*Vogues*] ran fourteen weeks and closed for the summer. I guess they had to close until J.J. stopped laughing at Mr. Lee's first musical attempt."*

Three costume sketches by designer Homer Conant for The Passing Show: *two chorus costumes from the 1917 edition ("Manhattan Cocktail Girl" and "Horse's Neck Girl") and an evening gown for female impersonator George Monroe from 1914. Like most revues of the period,* The Passing Show *often featured thematic outfits for its chorus girls. Shubert chorines were costumed to represent drinks, flowers, nuts, animals, seasons of the year, and various makes of automobile and denominations of currency. Female impersonators were popular revue attractions during the teens, and veteran performer George Monroe, who had appeared in Broadway drag roles as early as the 1890s, was featured in the 1914* Passing Show *as Little Buttercup, Queen of the Movies.*

Stars of The Passing Show: (below, left) *Trixie Friganza,
Eugene and Willie Howard, and Ernest Hare in "The Metropolitan Squawktette" number from the edition of 1912;*
(right) *the Howard brothers in a burlesque of Trilby, from the
show's 1915 edition; and an advertising flyer for* The Passing
Show of 1921, *featuring photographs of former stars who had
appeared at the Winter Garden, the home of the famous Shubert revue. The Howards, who were well known for their
Jewish comedy routines, began in vaudeville and eventually
gravitated to revue. They were great favorites of the Shuberts
and appeared in most editions of* The Passing Show *until
1922. The "Metropolitan Squawktette" was a burlesque of
Verdi's Rigoletto which was to become one of the Howard
brothers' most famous routines.*

the morning. Every time there was a backstage crisis, Allen was shoved out in front of the curtain to entertain the audience. In all, he appeared eighteen times that night.

The various editions of *The Passing Show* were unabashedly girlie revues, full of low comedy and novelty effects, and produced with an eye to the budget and to the taste of the Tired Business Man in the audience. Perhaps the most memorable contribution of *The Passing Show* over the years was the artists that it brought to the Winter Garden. J.J. had an extraordinary knack for spotting the kind of theatrical talent that caused lines at the box-office—especially if the performers had already been making money for other producers. He did not keep his artists very long because of his legendary temper and his lack of interest in paying top wages, but in retrospect it seems that half the stars in show business did a turn for him in one edition or another of *The Passing Show.* Willie and Eugene Howard were perennials. Marilyn Miller's first major appearance on Broadway was in the 1914 edition. Ed Wynn appeared in 1916, De Wolf Hopper the next year, and Fred and Adele Astaire in 1918. Later editions featured the famous Avon Comedy Four, Marie Dressler, Fred Allen, Ethel Shutta, George Jessel, Walter Woolf, and a chorus girl named Lucille Le Sueur, shortly to be known as Joan Crawford.

In addition to the emerging stars and the ever-present girls, the early *Passing Shows,* like most Shubert revues and musicals of the day, featured elaborate scenic devices. Several of them employed the new technology borrowed from the movie industry. Lee and J.J., for example, were in correspondence with Fred D. Thomas, a scene designer who specialized in motion picture effects on stage, such as a "San Francisco Fire Scene" and an "Elevated Train on the Brooklyn Bridge Scene." For the *Passing Show* of 1914, Thomas was hired to provide a "Trans-Atlantic Flight Scene" to close the first act, which involved three chorus girls boarding a dirigible and singing as it swept across the stage. For *The Whirl of the World,* another 1914 musical show, Thomas created a catastrophe at sea which involved a sinking ship and a skiff being rowed to the rescue. Three years later, in *The Show of Wonders,* another Shubert designer, Henri De Vries, would present a particularly novel and elaborate scene using film in which a group of sailors escaped from a submerged submarine.

It was in *The Whirl of the World*, that Broadway was first introduced to a composer whose work would become central to Lee and J.J.'s producing. Sigmund Romberg, a Hungarian, born in 1887, had wound up as a musician at Bustanoby's Restaurant, a well-known theatrical haunt at Thirty-ninth Street and Broadway. J.J. was impressed by some of Romberg's compositions and hired him for a new musical. At the time the young musician was also working on songs which would be interpolated into a 1915 Shubert musical at the Casino, *The Blue Paradise*. A recycled Viennese confection, like many Shubert productions before and after it, *The Blue Paradise* had been adapted for Broadway by Edgar Smith. The Shubert version, which ran for more than 350 performances, contained a number of the original songs by Viennese composer Edmund Eysler, but the majority of interpolations—including the lovely "Auf Wiedersehn"—were by Romberg.

The Shuberts were to use Romberg again for the 1917 *Maytime*, one of his best scores and a perennial favorite with stock and amateur producers through the 1950s. *Maytime* tells the story of a pair of young lovers who are unable to marry, but whose grandchildren eventually fall in love, marry, and realize their grandparents' thwarted hopes. *Maytime*, like *The Blue Paradise*, was a Viennese import, but because of growing anti-German feeling on the eve of World War I, the book was recast by librettist Rida Johnson Young, who set the story in America. Along with the Austrian setting, the entire score by Walter Kollo was thrown out and a completely new one by Romberg substituted. The new show, while basically in the Viennese operetta tradition, had many distinctly American touches and half a dozen first-rate songs, among them the immensely popular "Will You Remember?". It was a bonanza. So popular was the show that the new Shubert Theatre could not handle the crowds and a second company was installed near by at the Forty-fourth Street Theatre. (In a shrewd advertising ploy, Lee and J.J. later billed both companies on tour as the "entire New York cast.")

By the late teens the focus of the Broadway theatre district had clearly shifted to the Times Square area. Although the Shuberts continued to produce in other people's theatres outside the area—especially in the

The "Submarine F-7 Scene" from the second edition of The Show of Wonders, *1917. The spectacular twenty-minute sketch, which employed both elaborate stage technology and projected film, involved the torpedoing of the F-7 and the ultimate rescue of its crew. In the scene shown here, sailors gasp for breath as the submarine's air is exhausted, while divers descend from the flys to rescue them. At the end of the sketch, when the rescue was complete, an American flag was lowered into the scene and the audience stood up to sing the national anthem, accompanied by the theatre orchestra.*

Flyer for The Whirl of the World, *1914, Sigmund Romberg's first Broadway show; a photograph of the composer in middle age; manuscript of a Romberg song from* Robinson Crusoe, Jr., *1916; flyer for the successful* The Blue Paradise, *1915, a show with interpolations by Romberg. In his early years with the Shuberts, Romberg was a staff songwriter, replacing their former house composer Louis Hirsch. Romberg turned his hand to any kind of music required for Shubert revues and musicals, including incidental songs for such minor 1916 shows as* The Girl from Brazil *and* Follow Me, *with Florenz Ziegfeld's ex-wife Anna Held. It was with* Maytime *in 1917 that Romberg struck what historian Cecil Smith called the "vein of refined and warmly spontaneous lyricism for which he is still held in affection."*

WILLIE
HOWARD

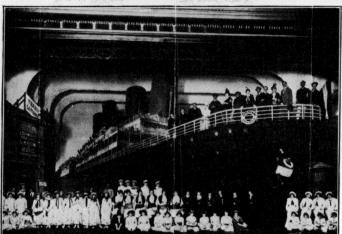

THE S. S. "VATERLAND" DEPARTING FROM HER DOCK

EUGENE
HOWARD

THE WHIRL OF THE WORLD

The New York Winter Garden's most spectacular extravaganza, popularly pronounced the most wonderful entertainment ever seen in Chicago.

COMPANY OF 125 HEADED BY
EUGENE AND WILLIE HOWARD

12 MAGNIFICENT SCENES
60 GORGEOUSLY GOWNED GIRLS
30 MELODIOUS SONG HITS

Photographic key sheet for Maytime, *1917, showing the principals in scenes from Act I. The production featured Peggy Wood as Ottillie Van Zandt, the daughter of an aristocratic Washington Square family, Douglas J. Wood as her snobbish cousin Claude, to whom she is engaged, and Charles Purcell as Richard Wayne, the apprentice with whom she is in love. As the Shubert play catalogue put it, "Richard insults Claude, and being discharged, takes his departure, declaring that he will return Ottillie's equal and marry her." In fact, it is their grandchildren who will finally marry in the last act, "aware that the thwarted hopes of their grandparents are being realized in themselves."*

case of minor shows which were not likely to attract much attention or much money—they increasingly centered their own theatre construction within a few blocks of the corner of Broadway and Forty-second Street. But it was Forty-fourth and Forty-fifth streets, between Broadway and Eighth Avenue, that were to become the "Shubert" streets and, to this day, the heart of the theatrical district. Between 1913 and 1917, Lee and J.J. built or bought no fewer than five houses there: the Weber and Fields Theatre (renamed by the Shuberts the Forty-fourth Street Theatre), the Sam S. Shubert, the Booth, the Plymouth, and the Broadhurst.

The Weber and Fields, on the south side of Forty-fourth Street where the rear of the *New York Times* printing plant stands today, was a large musical house designed by William Swasey. The theatre, complete with a roof garden and a basement cabaret, was built by the famous comedy team in 1913 during one of their periods of reconciliation. They found the house too costly and too unprofitable, however, and it shortly came into the hands of the Shuberts.

In the same year, Lee and J.J. built their own new theatre, the Sam S. Shubert, directly across from the Weber and Fields on Forty-fourth Street. The Shubert was designed by Henry Herts, member of a firm responsible for several early Broadway houses, and seated some 1400 spectators. In the lobby was the by now ubiquitous portrait of Sam, which Lee and J.J. placed in all their theatres. But the Shubert was conceived as a special memorial to Sam and as the surviving brothers'

A 1938 photograph of Lee and J.J.'s flagship theatre, the Sam S. Shubert, built in 1913 on West Forty-fourth Street. The architect of the Shubert, Henry B. Herts, was a founding partner of the firm of Herts and Tallant, which had previously created the designs for a number of important New York City theatres, including, in 1903, Daniel Frohman's Lyceum (now the home of the Shubert Archive) and Klaw and Erlanger's lavish New Amsterdam. The balconies at the Shubert are cantilevered to avoid columns which would interfere with the spectators' view of the stage, an engineering innovation which Herts pioneered at the New Amsterdam. Today the interior of the Shubert retains much of its elegant original plasterwork, as well as an unusual set of murals of classical subjects.

flagship house. Above it were some of the company's offices and Lee's penthouse apartment.

Lee's penthouse was in the tradition of living and working "over the store" which was common among such important theatre owners and producers as Belasco and Daniel Frohman. In later years, J.J. had a penthouse atop the Sardi Building, across the street from his brother, which serves today as the home of the Dramatists Guild. According to John Shubert, both Lee and J.J. were originally scheduled to move into the new Sardi Building, which they built in 1927. But Lee stayed put, on the other side of Forty-fourth Street, in quarters above the Shubert Theatre which he had previously shared as office space with J.J.

"The real reason behind Lee's reluctance to move his office staff," John said, "lay in the simple fact that Lee wanted plenty of distance between his brother and himself. The number and intensity of their arguments had increased constantly over the years, and it had become virtually impossible for the two men to work side by side on the same floor on the top of the Shubert Theatre. Lee reasoned that they would still see each other much too often even if they were separated by a whole floor in the new Sardi Building. But, a hundred and fifty feet of space between them, guarded by the asphalt of Forty-fourth Street and its consistently heavy traffic, seemed the ideal diplomatic barrier. So, Lee remained in his small circular room on top of the Shubert." The spartan little room, which exists more or less intact today, was described by Ruth Gordon in an interview as "really pink like a wild rose. So here's Mr. Lee Shubert, who runs the whole world," she said, "sitting in a pink office."

Running alongside the Shubert was the famous private alley that connected Forty-fourth and Forty-fifth streets. At its northern end, directly behind the Shubert, Lee and Winthrop Ames (Lee's partner in the New Theatre fiasco) built the handsome Booth Theatre. Like the Shubert Theatre, which shares the same façade on Shubert Alley, the Booth was built in 1913 by architect Henry Herts. The Booth, conceived as a small dramatic house, was only half the size of its southern neighbor. It was named for the famous Shakespearean actor Edwin Booth and was decorated with Booth memorabilia. Just next

A room in Lee Shubert's apartment and office suite above the Shubert Theatre, and the living room of J.J.'s apartment across Forty-fourth Street, on top of the Sardi Building. J.J.'s office was on a lower floor of the same building. The portrait over the fireplace is of J.J.'s son John, who would take over the company in later years. The room remains more or less intact today, although the portrait now hangs in the theatre collection of the Museum of the City of New York. In Lee's suite, traces of the elaborate original decoration may still be seen in several rooms, including a large formal dining room which once featured a working fountain and a minstrels' gallery.

Two views of Shubert Alley, the private street that still runs between Forty-fourth Street and Forty-fifth Street, just west of Broadway. The photograph looking north from the Shubert Theatre was made in 1959 during the run of Take Me Along; the second photograph, looking south from the Booth Theatre, was probably made at the same time. The low building across the Alley from the two theatres had replaced a bus station, which once filled the eastern part of the space. The bus station, in turn, had taken the place of late nineteenth-century brownstones from the period when the block was part of a residential neighborhood. Just to the east was the famous Astor Hotel, a Broadway landmark from 1904 until 1968.

A 1964 photograph of the Booth Theatre, built in 1913. The Booth is a small dramatic house, with a beautifully paneled Tudor-inspired auditorium, on West Forty-fifth Street at the north end of Shubert Alley. The Booth stands back-to-back with the Shubert Theatre along Shubert Alley. Henry Herts's double exterior for the Booth and the Shubert, designed in the "Venetian Renaissance" style, resulted in what appears to be a single huge building, facing on the Alley, with a rather restrained brick and terra-cotta façade. The Shuberts' Plymouth Theatre, by architect Herbert Krapp, may be seen just to the west of the Booth, at the right of the photograph.

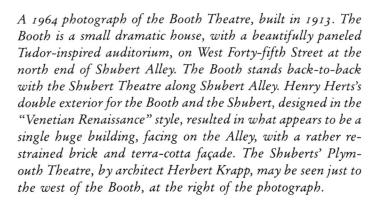

door on Forty-fifth Street was another collaboration with an independent producer, the Plymouth Theatre. Arthur Hopkins, like Ames, was a serious man of the theatre with an interest in creating first-class productions of the classics and of new "uncommercial" plays. During the first several years after its opening in 1917, Hopkins—often with Shubert backing—was to produce a number of important classic revivals and innovative new plays there.

The Plymouth was designed by a young theatre architect named Herbert Krapp, a onetime apprentice with Herts and Tallant. Over the years, Krapp, a solid designer and acoustician, was to become, in effect, the Shuberts' "official" architect and the designer of more than twenty Broadway houses, both for Lee and J.J. and for other theatre owners. On Forty-fourth Street, back to back with the Plymouth, Krapp built the Broadhurst Theatre, also in 1917. It was a third Shubert venture with an outside producer, in this case, the playwright-manager George Broadhurst. In his day Broadhurst was a popular writer of commercial comedies and melodramas, as well as an experienced producer of other writers' works. In the late teens, the

Herbert J. Krapp, in 1905, about the time he completed his apprenticeship with Herts and Tallant and joined the firm, which handled many important theatre-building projects. In later years, he struck out on his own as an architect specializing in theatres. Krapp, a graduate of New York's Cooper Union, was a talented acoustician, who became widely known for the care with which he worked out the details of auditorium design. For the most part, his strength lay with the practical aspects of theatre architecture rather than with the aesthetic, and a number of his Broadway houses from the teens and twenties are still in constant use today. Krapp's pragmatic approach suited Lee and J.J. perfectly, and although he worked for a number of different clients during his career, he became the Shuberts' house architect.

Advertisement for Justine Johnstone in Over the Top, *a 1917 Shubert revue; and a Homer Conant design for Betty Pierce in the "Justine Johnstone Rag" number, from the same show. Johnstone, known as "America's loveliest woman," was a former photographer's model and Follies girl. Lee Shubert, Johnstone's "protector," in the phrase of the day, aggressively promoted her career as a musical comedy star. But she shortly left the musical theatre, married— and later divorced—producer Walter Wanger, and had a somewhat limited career as a comedienne on stage and in the motion pictures. Later still she abandoned the theatre altogether for work in medical research.*

theatre named for him housed several of Broadhurst's plays and many by other playwrights, including the highly successful Shubert-produced *39 East,* a comedy by Rachel Crothers that opened in the theatre in March 1919, with Allison Skipworth, Henry Hull, and Constance Binney.

American involvement in World War I had spawned a number of patriotic Broadway shows toward the end of the teens, among them a 1917 Romberg revue at the Forty-fourth Street Roof, conceived as a vehicle for Justine Johnstone, a former Ziegfeld showgirl. The show, *Over the Top,* was a mishmash of numbers composed by Romberg and Herman Timberg, and included an "Aviator Number" and the "Justine Johnstone Rag." Performing with the star in their first Broadway roles were Fred and Adele Astaire, who would shortly be seen in *The Passing Show of 1918.*

Lee was hopelessly smitten with Johnstone, for whom he planned all sorts of tours and vehicles, including a road tour of *Girl O'Mine,* a small musical that opened at the Shuberts' new Bijou on Forty-fifth Street in January 1918. The show, about an American girl's adventures in Paris, was co-produced by the Shuberts and Elisabeth Marbury. Marbury was a prominent agent, a society figure, and the guiding spirit behind the small-scale, artistically integrated Princess Theatre musicals being produced at F. Ray Comstock's intimate playhouse on Thirty-ninth Street, which was owned in part by the Shuberts. The Princess shows featured the music of Jerome Kern, with books and lyrics by Guy Bolton and P.G. Wodehouse. *Girl O'Mine* was conceived essentially in the same spirit as the Kern-Bolton-Wodehouse musicals. But a poor score by Frank Tours led to a disappointing six-week run, in spite of a relatively strong book and the appearance of the great Irish-American vaudeville comic Frank Fay as a prizefighter-turned-bartender.

Meanwhile, J.J.'s marriage to Catherine had ended in a messy divorce. In 1916 a newspaper article had linked J.J. to two women in a show that was trying out in New Haven. As a result of the article, Catherine and J.J., who had been incompatible for some time, now became loudly and irreconcilably estranged. The papers were filled

J.J. Shubert on shipboard during the mid-teens, with his mother Catherine, his son John (in the sailor suit), and two unidentified children, possibly John's cousins Sylvia Wolf and Milton Shubert; and a children's party from the same period. John Shubert is at the far right of the party photograph. John, who would spend most of his time with his mother, after her divorce from J.J., was to have relatively little contact with his father for many years. As a young man, he went to work for J.J. with a certain trepidation. "John Shubert," an old employee said, "felt the pressure and expectations from his father and tried to please him." But the relationship between the two always remained strained and difficult.

with news and speculations about an upcoming divorce and about J.J.'s legendary roving eye. In February 1917 the pair were divorced in Buffalo, New York. The event was carefully orchestrated by long-time Shubert attorney William Klein to minimize publicity. In spite of J.J.'s vehement protests, Catherine got a generous alimony settlement and full custody of their son. As John Shubert would later recall it, he was to grow up as a virtual stranger to his father.

IV
THE TWENTIES: BOOM ON BROADWAY

As I look back on it now, we must never have stopped to think, but to tell the truth, we hardly had time for that. Why at one point we had thirty-six of our attractions touring the key cities. Nine of them were "Student Prince" companies which sent us in a profit of over one million dollars one season . . . We held the whip in those days, too, and I must confess we cracked it now and then.

LEE SHUBERT

In 1919 most of the theatres on Broadway were closed down by a massive strike. Six years earlier, professional actors had become so concerned about the power of managers that they formed the Actors' Equity Association to protect their interests. Since then Equity had been attempting, without much success, to increase wages and improve working conditions. Producers and theatre owners—Lee and J.J. among them—were unenthusiastic about change, and relations between Broadway management and labor grew increasingly strained. On August 6, 1919, after years of fruitless negotiations, Equity at last called a strike that crippled the theatre business in New York and on the road for some four weeks. The Shuberts, with characteristic stubbornness, continued to run the Winter Garden during the early days of the strike, using company executives as backstage and house staff and presenting a hodge-podge show based on several of their previous revues. Meanwhile, they sued Equity and a number of its individual members for half a million dollars, based on their estimate of the money the company was losing during the strike period. The case was thrown out of court, and by September 6, Equity had won the strike and was officially recognized as the legal bargaining agent for performers. It was the beginning of years of skirmishes between the Shuberts and the actors' union. But in one sense at least Lee and J.J. had to come out ahead—it was the strike that gained them Eddie Cantor.

Cantor was born Isidore Itzkowitz on the Lower East Side of New York in 1892. In 1916 he had graduated from vaudeville to a slot in Florenz Ziegfeld's *Midnight Frolics*. During the next three seasons

Eddie Cantor in Make It Snappy, *1922, at the Winter Garden, his second show for the Shuberts after leaving Ziegfeld's* Follies. *Like Jolson, Cantor was a superb entertainer, although the exact nature of his talent remains hard to pin down. As Marjorie Farnsworth suggested in her history of* The Follies, *"technically speaking he was neither a singer nor a dancer. It was the delivery and timing that did it. He had a feverish, infectious gaiety that swept across the footlights and carried everyone with it, and back of it was a kind of joyous tenderness that went to the heart." Cantor did excellent work for Lee and J.J., but they had little in common. "Mr. Ziegfeld was class," he once wrote, "the Shuberts were just showbusiness."*

Ziegfeld put the young singer-comedian in his *Follies,* where he made a decided hit. But Cantor, a strong union sympathizer, walked out of the 1919 *Ziegfeld Follies* in support of the actors' strike. Ziegfeld fired him and he promptly joined forces with the Shuberts. Unlike Jolson, who was in his element working with J.J., Cantor seemed never to have been truly comfortable with the Shuberts and made no bones about the fact that he felt their work inferior to Ziegfeld's. Actually, as soon as he and Ziegfeld were able to patch up their differences, Cantor left the Shuberts and returned to work for his former boss. But the Shuberts managed to star their new acquisition in several popular shows during the early twenties.

Among these was a cabaret show called *The Midnight Rounders,* which Lee and J.J. presented in the rooftop theatre at the Century during the summer of 1920. Cantor also appeared in another show, *Broadway Brevities of 1920,* in which the Shuberts probably had a financial interest, although they were not listed as producers. At least part of the money to finance the show came from the great black comedian, Bert Williams, who, along with his friend Cantor, had also left Ziegfeld and the *Follies* and had joined the Shuberts. The show, which opened in September at the Winter Garden, contained a Cantor sketch, "The Dentist's Office," that was a direct affront to Ziegfeld, since it was virtually identical to one the comedian had performed in the 1919 *Follies.* Ziegfeld sued, and the sketch was removed from the show. *Broadway Brevities,* which ran for a decent but unimpressive thirteen weeks, was to be Williams's last Broadway appearance. His health had been poor for some time, and in February 1922, during an out-of-town tryout for a Shubert comedy called *Under the Bamboo Tree,* Williams came down with pneumonia. He died in New York early in March. Cantor, meanwhile, was just at the beginning of a remarkably successful career as an entertainer, and his final show for the Shuberts would help to clinch his success.

Make It Snappy was a Winter Garden show which opened in April 1922 and featured Cantor in his famous Max the Tailor routine and in several other comedy numbers. The public was impressed with Cantor and so were the critics, one of whom pointed out that "Al Jolson now has a rival." Jolson was more than aware of the fact and seems to have viewed the benign and decent Cantor as a threat to his own

The great black star Bert Williams during tryouts in 1921 for his last production, Under the Bamboo Tree. *He was touring the show for the Shuberts at the time of his death in 1922, at the age of forty-seven. Williams had toured for Lee and J.J. once before, in 1909, in* Mr. Lode of Koal. *At the time, the manager of the Garrick Theatre in St. Louis had telegraphed to J.J. in panic about the booking: "Positively will injure us greatly opening with Bert Williams. Press and public sentiment vigorously opposed to colored attractions playing Garrick. We have much at stake here." J.J. was uncharacteristically measured in his response to the manager. "I don't think we will make any mistake in playing the Williams show there," he replied. "I think you take matters of this sort too seriously."*

career. He need not have worried. With the backing of the Shuberts, Jolson had become the biggest star in America. And while Cantor performed at the Winter Garden, Jolson was ensconced in an immensely successful show at a theatre named for him and totally financed by Lee and J.J.

The Jolson Theatre, on Seventh Avenue between Fifty-eighth and

Two "Vampire" costumes for chorus girls, Make It Snappy, *1922. Make It* Snappy *also contained a number in which chorus members were dressed as roses. The designs are by Cora MacGeachy, a frequent contributor to Shubert shows, as well as to revues by other producers, during the teens and twenties. MacGeachy is known to have created costumes for several editions of the* Passing Show, *the* Ziegfeld Follies, *the* Music Box Revue, *and George White's* Scandals. *Yet, like many of the costume designers of the era, she remains an obscure figure. In no small part this is because the contributions of costume designers were more or less taken for granted by producers and were generally given little publicity in programs and press releases.*

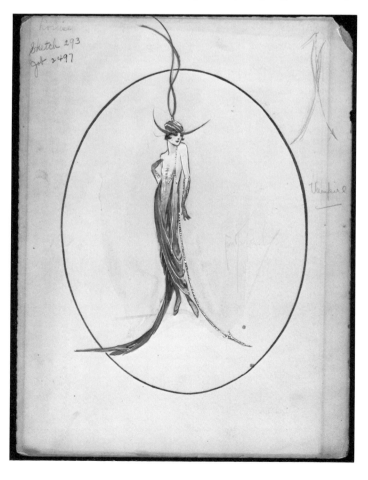
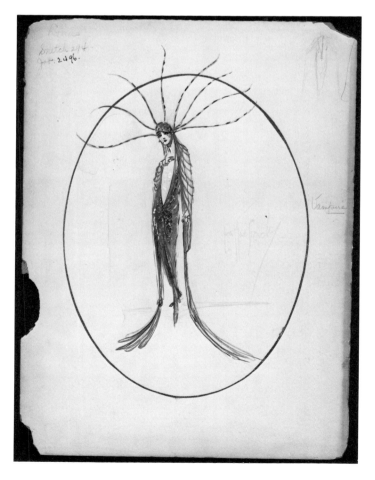

Fifty-ninth streets, had opened in October 1921 with *Bombo*, the Jolson vehicle to end them all. *Bombo* was a sensation, although certainly not because of the book and lyrics by Harold Atteridge. The show was yet another of the disconnected Winter Garden-style epics which had served Jolson so well for the preceding decade. Once again, Jolson was the black-face character Gus. This time, however, Gus was transformed, in a dream sequence, into Bombo, Christopher Columbus's servant. Bombo convinces Queen Isabella to finance his master's voyage to the New World, encourages his shipmates when

Sheet music cover for "Toot, Toot, Tootsie," from Al Jolson's Shubert hit Bombo, *1921, a song which he would reintroduce in the first important American sound film,* The Jazz Singer, *1927; and Jolson, in blackface, with two chorus girls from the* Bombo *company. Shortly after* Bombo, *Jolson left Lee and J.J., to their extreme displeasure, after a long string of successful and very lucrative shows. He would return to the Shuberts twice more over the years, for* Big Boy, *a 1925 hit show in which his blackface character, Gus, wins the Derby, and the unsuccessful* The Wonder Bar, *in 1931, with Jolson in a whiteface role. Jolson's final Broadway musical,* Hold On to Your Hats, *1941, was not produced by the Shuberts, but it played in Shubert houses in New York and on the road.*

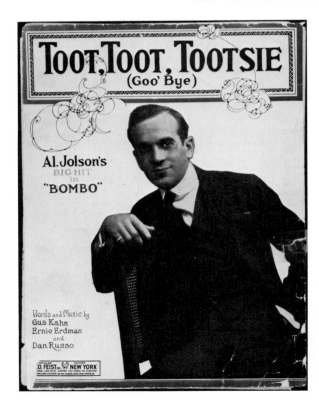

their expedition seems futile, and arranges matters with the natives when Columbus reaches the West Indies—all to an undistinguished score by Romberg. As in the Winter Garden shows, the really effective songs were the show-stopping interpolations created for Jolson: "April Showers," "Toot, Toot, Tootsie!," and "California, Here I Come," the last of which was introduced on the road.

Bombo ran for more than 200 performances in New York and had an immensely successful road tour, with sixteen weeks in Chicago alone. But Jolson, who had gone on to other things, never appeared again in the theatre named for him. Typically, Lee and J.J. ultimately changed the theatre's name and hung on to it. They lost the house during the Depression, along with a number of other theatres, but regained it in 1944. In later years, it, like many Broadway theatres, became a television studio. The Jolson was finally torn down in 1962 and an apartment house built on the site.

In 1920 the brothers decided to re-enter vaudeville. A dozen years earlier they had joined with Klaw and Erlanger in an attempt to break the virtual monopoly in the field held by Keith's United Booking Office. Now they faced Keith once again, this time on their own, aided by Arthur Klein, a former Keith employee who had been recruited to head the Shubert operation. Shubert Advanced Vaudeville, founded in the spring of 1920, was to operate in thirty-six cities across the country, using existing Shubert theatres and houses leased from other owners. At the outset the brothers claimed to be considering some seventy-five major attractions, including Fanny Brice, Weber and Fields, Nora Bayes, Fred and Adele Astaire, the Dolly Sisters, Gertrude Hoffman, Eva Tanguay, the Sousa Band, and the Fokine Ballet.

Ticket prices ranged from twenty-five cents to one-dollar top, and the shows played two a day, seven days a week. In New York and other cities with Sunday blue laws, the Sunday presentations were labeled "concerts." Typically, the shows presented on the Shubert circuit were standard vaudeville, with the addition of some newsreel and cartoon films and tabloid versions of popular musicals and revues. As John Shubert noted, the Shubert vaudeville format was basically borrowed from old minstrel shows, which presented a number

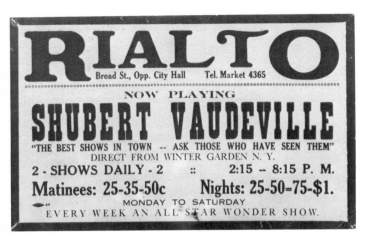

Two advertising flyers for Shubert Vaudeville during the early twenties. Gertrude Hoffmann, whose picture appears in the second flyer, was a vaudeville dancer turned dance director— and a somewhat unusual character. Hoffmann gained a certain notoriety for a torrid "Dance of the Seven Veils" number and for her involvement in a highly publicized lawsuit in which she was accused of stealing material from dancer Maud Allen. Over the years, the Gertrude Hoffmann Girls were featured in a number of Lee and J.J.'s musical shows, as was another company, the Albertina Rasch Girls, led by a former Viennese ballet dancer. The so-called Musicomedies mentioned in the flyer were mostly one-act versions of musical shows previously produced by Lee and J.J. in New York or on the road.

of individual acts followed by a so-called "after-piece," a play featuring entertainers who had appeared earlier in the show. Fred Allen, for example, recalled in his autobiography that when he played Shubert vaudeville he was "assigned to a unit that starred Lew Fields in a condensation of *Snapshots*, a show he had done on Broadway." The first part of the evening "consisted of five acts of vaudeville: the Arco Brothers, A. Robins, Yvette, Fred Allen, and McConnell and Simpson." Following the intermission, Fields's *Snapshots* was presented in a tabloid version as an hour-long revue.

Competition was fierce, and in October 1923 the Shuberts sued the Keith and Orpheum circuits for "unlawful combination in restraint of trade." By March 1924, Arthur Klein had resigned and Shubert Vaudeville was once again out of business. In part because of their re-entry into the field, Lee and J.J. had begun to search vaudeville and burlesque for potential comic and musical talent for their legitimate

Shubert Vaudeville during the early 1920s: an advertisement for a vaudeville bill; and a photograph of sandwich-board men advertising Halloween vaudeville performances at the Shubert-Crescent Theatre in Brooklyn. The bizarre sandwich-board men are typical of the sort of uninhibited promotion dear to the hearts of the Shubert Press Department of the period. The vaudeville advertisement shows a typical bill, made up of a combination of variety acts and an afterpiece—one of the Shuberts' so-called Musicomedies. The afterpiece in this case was a shortened version ("condensed from hours to minutes") of a reasonably popular but undistinguished 1918 show The Kiss Burglar.

shows. Within a few years they would successfully move into their revues and musicals such important vaudevillians as Fred Stone, Ed Wynn, the Marx Brothers, Victor Moore, Bert Lahr, and Eddie Dowling.

The early twenties was a highly successful time for Lee and J.J. as producers of musical theatre. In 1920, for example, they had staged a lucrative revival of the 1900 hit *Florodora.* Opening in April at the Century, the show was revamped with topical material and a number of turn-of-the-century songs which had not been in the original production. The story, about a conspiracy to rob the heroine of her rights to Florodora, a Philippine island, was as inconsequential as ever. But the public still adored the show's famous double sextet (six men and six women)—and especially the sextet's great hit, "Tell Me, Pretty Maiden."

Lee and J.J. had been in the cabaret business in a limited way since the early teens when they opened the Palais de Danse at the Winter Garden. Over the years, several of their houses would contain theatre-restaurants designed for the presentation of small musical revues, often with an adjacent dance floor for patrons. The Shuberts' New Theatre on Central Park West—by 1920 known as the Century—had been built with a palm garden restaurant on its roof, which had been used only sporadically over the years. In the mid-teens, however, the space had been turned into a cabaret, featuring revues presented by choreographer Ned Wayburn and later by Florenz Ziegfeld, whose scene designer Joseph Urban remodeled the space.

Beginning in July 1920, Lee and J.J. put a pair of revues into the cabaret, now known as the Century Promenade. Their brief nine o'clock show was called *The Century Revue:* it was followed by *The Midnight Rounders* with Cantor, at 11:30, a longer and more elaborate entertainment rather on the order of *The Passing Show.* Both appeared in a second edition in 1921, and the full-length *Midnight Rounders* later toured on its own. Because the dance craze of the teens had ended, and because Prohibition had become the law of the land, times were bad for cabaret entertainment. Audiences frustrated by a cabaret that offered no liquor sought out the new speakeasies, a

"Tell Me, Pretty Maiden," the famous sextet number, from J.J.'s *1920 revival of the 1900 Broadway success* Florodora. *The show, padded out with a certain amount of new material, was generally quite well received. But, as the* Post *critic wrote about opening night, "the sextet was the thing which is depended upon for the success of the revival, as it was in the original production, and there was an air of waiting for it in the house." In fact, there turned out to be three sextets this time, one in modern dress, another in turn-of-the-century costume, and a third made up entirely of children, including a young performer named Milton Berle. The gimmick was extremely popular, and J.J., unwilling to let a good premise go unenhanced, appears to have added a fourth sextet to a summer Shubert revival of the show during the thirties.*

Advertisement for one of the countless road tours of the *1921 Sigmund Romberg–Dorothy Donnelly* operetta Blossom Time; *and a costume sketch for the show by William Weaver, a popular designer of Broadway shows and Metropolitan Opera productions, and a specialist in period costumes. Critic Brooks Atkinson pointed out that "Broadway gave up the cloying past reluctantly. For years, revivals of* The Student Prince *and* Blossom Time *kept appearing out of nowhere." But the tours continued to make money, in no small part because they were done on the cheap. Broadway folklore has it that there are still lost companies of* Blossom Time *touring endlessly somewhere in the Middle West.*

number of which provided dance floors and small-scale variety entertainments along with their bootleg alcohol. As a result, Lee and J.J.
turned part of the rooftop space into a conventional small theatre,
with seats instead of tables and chairs. It was there that they presented the final Century revue, *The Mimic World* of 1921, which included
the somewhat exotic combination of Cliff Edwards ("Ukulele Ike")
and Mae West.

In September of 1921, Lee and J.J. would mount a musical show
that was to be among their greatest hits, *Blossom Time*. The fictionalized biography of Franz Schubert, which used the composer's
themes as the basis for its songs, had been created several years before
by the Viennese composer Heinrich Berté. Berté's show (known in
Austria as *Das Dreimäderlhaus* and in England as *Lilac Time*) had
been a great success throughout Europe. But the American adapters,
Sigmund Romberg and Dorothy Donnelly, had their own ideas about
the story and about the Schubert themes to be used in the show. Their
version was a radical revision and much of Berté's work was
discarded.

In the new version of the operetta, which ran for a total of almost
600 performances on Broadway and played endlessly on the road,
Franz Schubert is engaged to ghostwrite a song for an elderly nobleman, Count Scharntoff. The Count pays Schubert so well that the
composer is able to stage a feast for his friends, including young
Baron Franz Schober. Two young women, Fritzi and Kitzi, have
come to the party to meet two of Schubert's friends who are their
admirers. With them is their chaperone, Mitzi. The girls' father,
Kranz, has got wind of their meeting, however, and is on patrol
outside the door. Schober plies Kranz with wine and flattery and
eventually talks him into giving permission for his daughters to marry
the two young men.

The second act takes place at the wedding festivities, which are
being held at Kranz's house. Schubert writes a love song to Mitzi (the
famous "Song of Love," based on a theme from the *Unfinished Symphony*), but he is too shy to sing it to her. He asks Schober to do it
instead. Schober agrees, but in the heat of the moment, he confesses
to Mitzi that he is in love with her himself. Mitzi reciprocates his
feelings. Schubert is heartbroken and turns to his music for consola-

tion. In the third act, he is too ill to attend a performance of his latest symphony. Mitzi appears in Schubert's rooms and professes her love for him, but he realizes that it is really Schober the young woman loves. In the final scene, Schubert's friends return from the triumphant performance of his symphony to congratulate the dying composer on his great success.

While *Sally, Irene and Mary* did not have the tremendous reception of *Blossom Time*, it was a gratifying box-office success for Lee and J.J. The show, which appeared at the Casino early in September of 1922, owed a considerable debt to a fabulously successful Ziegfeld musical of 1920, *Sally,* which had starred Marilyn Miller and featured a book by Guy Bolton and music by Jerome Kern and Victor Herbert. The Shubert knock-off had begun life as a vaudeville sketch featuring Eddie Dowling, who would appear in and direct many of Lee and J.J.'s shows over the years. Although *Sally, Irene and Mary* received

An ex-Follies *performer, Eddie Dowling, wrote the book for* Sally, Irene and Mary *(1922) with Shubert House writer Cyrus Wood, basing the show on a sketch he had developed originally for Shubert Vaudeville at the Winter Garden. Dowling was also a director and producer, a composer and lyricist, and a virtuoso song-and-dance man. He is probably best remembered today, however, for his serious acting roles, especially as Tom Wingfield in Tennessee Williams's* The Glass Menagerie *(1945). Dowling worked with Lee and J.J. a number of times over the years and, indeed, seems to have been that comparative rarity, an actor they actually considered to be a friend. To confuse the issue, another Eddie Dowling—Edward Duryea Dowling—was a close friend of John Shubert and directed a number of shows for the company from the thirties through the early fifties.*

Stage design, artist unknown, showing the Provincetown Playhouse and other Greenwich Village landmarks, probably from an edition of the Greenwich Village Follies. *Originally the show was a miniaturized Village version of the sort of revue popular on Broadway during the teens. In its early days it possessed an unusual ambience that one show business veteran called "kind of off-Broadway—semi-amateur." The Shuberts quickly spotted the show's potential and moved it uptown. Editions of the* Greenwich Village Follies *during the twenties became more elaborate than the original, but the Shuberts continued to trade on the popular notion that "anything goes in the Village," and to spoof all of its more colorful institutions, from berets and batiks to free love and speakeasies.*

lukewarm reviews, the rather bathetic story about immigrant Irish on their way up from the Lower East Side caught the public's fancy and ran for the entire 1922–1923 season.

At the other end of the season's spectrum was the rather arch and extremely popular Viennese operetta, *The Lady in Ermine,* which featured one of Lee and J.J.'s favorites, musical comedy star Walter Woolf. The complicated plot involved the capture of a castle, a group of stranded La Scala ballet girls and their comic manager, Baron Sprotti-Sprotti, and the castle's mistress, with whom the head of the

invading forces falls in love. The show's hit song was a Romberg interpolation, "When Hearts Are Young."

A few nights after the opening of *Sally, Irene and Mary,* a borrowed attraction of a different sort, *The Greenwich Village Follies,* opened at the Shubert Theatre. Like many other producers—the Shuberts among them—John Murray Anderson had appropriated Florenz Ziegfeld's revue premise and adapted it to his own theatrical vision—in this case, one strongly influenced by New York's bohemian community around Washington Square. Beginning in 1919 at a tiny theatre on Sheridan Square in Greenwich Village, Anderson produced a number of amusing pocket-sized revues under the title *Greenwich Village Follies.* From the start his work attracted the attention of the Shuberts, who had been immensely successful with the revue format and who were always looking for a way to beat Ziegfeld at his own game. The early editions of the show were swiftly moved uptown by Lee and J.J., who began to retailor them to their own tastes. By 1922, Anderson's *Follies* had become very much a conventional Broadway revue, with a front curtain by Reginald Marsh and sets by the popular French designer Erté. The closing number, "Greenwich Village Nights," featured Bert Savoy, the last of the great female impersonators to appear on Broadway until the 1950s, and the supposed inspiration for Mae West's extravagant stage persona.

It was *Artists and Models,* however, that was to prove to be the most enduring Shubert revue of the twenties and thirties. The first edition, which opened in August 1923, was basically a response to the all-stops-out girlie-show approach to revue being developed by

Four designs for chorus girl costumes by Howard Greer, probably for the 1922 edition of the Greenwich Village Follies. *Greer would later be an important fashion designer. The 1922 edition was among the most interesting in terms of design. In addition to Greer's contributions, there were costume designs by Erté, as well as scenery by the talented designer Cleon Throckmorton and the artist Reginald Marsh. Marsh's front curtain for the show was a kind of panoramic view of Greenwich Village, complete with portraits of many of its most famous denizens, including Max Eastman, Edmund Wilson, John Sloan, Eugene O'Neill, Susan Glaspell, and Edna St. Vincent Millay. Marsh placed himself on the roof of the Provincetown Playhouse, and Zelda Fitzgerald was shown diving into the Washington Square fountain.*

Advertising flyer for Artists and Models; *proof of an advertisement for the show on the road; and a photograph of the chorus from the 1927 edition.* Artists and Models *was built around the display of scantily clad chorus girls. Their charms were generally promoted with a certain lack of subtlety. As the newspaper proof suggests, Chicago audiences attending the 1926 edition of* Artists and Models *were asked to guess the combined weight of the "18 GERTRUDE HOFFMAN GIRLS, whose 18 beautiful bodies are the 'Talk of Chicago' . . . the Hoffman Girls will be officially weighed on stage in presence of the audience."*

Broadway producer Earl Carroll. A decade earlier, Lee and J.J. had challenged Ziegfeld's successful *Follies* with *The Passing Show*. Now *The Passing Show* was in decline and they set out to borrow Carroll's emphasis on nudity and near-nudity. His show, *Vanities*, which opened earlier in the summer, had been highly successful. The results of the Shubert imitation were mixed. Comedian Frank Fay served as master of ceremonies for *Artists and Models* of 1923, which was light on costuming and even lighter on content. The critics stressed the show's vulgarity. In spite of the reviews—or perhaps because of them—audiences came to *Artists and Models,* which ran for more than 300 performances, quite enough to justify its continuation the next year. Over the years, the show would appear in half a dozen editions.

Capitalizing on their success with *The Passing Show* and *Artists and Models,* the Shuberts had also attempted a new summer girlie revue, *Gay Paree,* in 1925. During a recent European tour, J.J. had seen the Folies Bergère in Paris. In August, Lee and J.J. brought out what may have been a Folies-inspired show, although in fact *Gay Paree* seems not to have had much to do with France or the French, and was built around sketches written by Harold Atteridge for rube comic Chic Sale, famous for his outhouse humor. But the show featured a chorus of Folies-style showgirls and it ran for almost 200 performances. A second edition, also with Sale, would appear during the next summer at the Winter Garden.

The Dream Girl, Victor Herbert's final Broadway operetta, gave the Shuberts a run of fifteen weeks at the Ambassador during the 1924–

1925 season. Based on a popular play called *The Road to Yesterday,* it concerned a young woman who falls asleep in twentieth-century London and, in her dreams, finds herself in the same city 300 years earlier. Part of the show's modest appeal came from an excellent cast: Fay Bainter, the comedian Billy B. Van, and Walter Woolf, who sang the title song, which was to become an American standard. *The Dream Girl* was adapted by the ever-present Rida Johnson Young and Harold Atteridge and contained a number of interpolated songs by Romberg.

During the same season, Lee and J.J. managed to turn yet another of their revivals into a theatrical bonanza. This time it was a musical version of *Old Heidelberg,* the warhorse in which Richard Mansfield had performed for years and which the Shuberts had produced in 1903 and again in 1910. The show, which opened in December of 1924, was rewritten for the musical stage by the talented Dorothy Donnelly, with music by Romberg, and starred a young German singer, Ilse Marvenga. The Donnelly-Romberg version, originally called *The Student Prince in Heidelberg* and later simply *The Student Prince,* was fairly close to the German original, although Donnelly grafted on a bittersweet ending.

The story is quintessential operetta material. Prince Karl Franz of Karlsberg, his kindly tutor, and his comic valet arrive in Heidelberg. There, incognito, the prince is to spend a year studying at the university. At the inn where they take up residence, he meets his landlord's beautiful daughter Kathie and joins a student cadet corps. Kathie and Karl Franz fall deeply in love, but he is called away to the bedside of his grandfather, the king, who is desperately ill. While he is in Karlsberg, the prince is forced, for political reasons, to enter a loveless marriage with Princess Margaret. Later, Karl Franz, who has become king after his grandfather's death, returns to Heidelberg for a final farewell to Kathie and his carefree student days. As the curtain falls, the prince and the innkeeper's daughter vow never to forget their love for one another.

The Student Prince represents Romberg at his finest. It is filled with charming tunes, among them "Golden Days," the "Students' Marching Song," the "Drinking Song," and the classic "Deep in My Heart, Dear." The show was a smash hit, running more than 600 performances on Broadway, and playing endlessly on the road.

An exotic fan number from the 1926 edition of the Shubert revue Gay Paree; *a portrait of humorist Chic Sale, who appeared in the 1925 and 1926 Broadway versions; and the "Gay Paree Girls," a photograph from the 1928 touring edition of the show. Sale, who played earthy rural types, was a famous vaudeville headliner, who consistently stopped the show at the Palace. For the most part, he wrote his own material. In the 1926 edition of* Gay Paree, *however, Sale offered "He Knew Lincoln," a sketch based on a story by Ida M. Tarbell, about Billy Brown, a friend of Abraham Lincoln, who recalls a visit with the President. Three years later Sale would achieve immortality of a sort with publication of his pamphlet "The Specialist," the reminiscences of a small-town privy builder, which sold more than two million copies.*

Sheet music for "Deep in My Heart, Dear," from the Shuberts' immensely popular operetta The Student Prince; and a 1924 photograph, showing Ilsa Marvenga as the innkeeper's daughter, Kathie, with the show's male chorus in the famous "Drinking Song" scene. Marvenga would play the starring soprano role of Kathie more than 3000 times on Broadway and in road companies. Like Blossom Time, The Student Prince was a perennial on the road. It was sometimes remarked that Lee and J.J. treated the casting and production values of these touring shows with a certain casualness. An old actor recalls that when he joined the chorus of a Student Prince tour, "the Shuberts gave me a beer mug and a road map, and the rest was history."

Eventually, there were nine companies of *The Student Prince* throughout the country, and, like *Blossom Time*, it became a synonym for the down-at-the-heels touring musical. Yet, its appeal in the United States seems perennial. In later years, the musical became—along with *Blossom Time* and *The Firefly*—one of the most popular offerings of the Century Library, the Shuberts' play-leasing operation. Today it remains a favorite with amateur groups around the country, and still receives a fair number of professional productions—perhaps the only Shubert show to survive the years as a hit.

In the mid-twenties, Lee and J.J.—undoubtedly at Lee's insistence—were continuing to produce a few fairly sophisticated straight plays, including Noel Coward's *Hay Fever* in October of 1925. In the same month, on his own, Lee presented *Man with a Load of*

Stock costume for Lutz, valet to Prince Karl Franz in The Student Prince. *Over the years, Lee and J.J. built up a huge costume collection in a warehouse on West Sixty-first Street. They usually drew on these stock costumes for their touring productions, as well as operating a costume rental service known as Stage Costumes, Inc. Stage Costumes did a considerable business with amateur theatre groups, schools, and summer stock companies, especially those doing old Shubert scripts. Producers could rent all the costumes for such shows as* Florodora, Maytime, *and* My Maryland. *But Stage Costumes, Inc. ("THE WORLD'S LARGEST WARDROBE of Sanitary AUTHENTIC THEATRICAL COSTUMES for MUSICAL SHOWS, REVUES, PAGEANTS, MINSTRELS, MASQUERADES, Etc.") could satisfy almost any request, as long as the client was not too fussy.*

Mischief, by English dramatist and critic Ashley Dukes, starring the popular actress Ruth Chatterton. And in April of the 1925–1926 season, Lee offered J.M. Barrie's classic comedy *What Every Woman Knows* at the tiny Bijou Theatre on Forty-fifth Street. In the cast was Helen Hayes, playing her first leading role on Broadway.

One of the more interesting plays came from the pen of young Broadway actor, James Gleason, who had decided to turn playwright. Gleason and his co-author, Richard Taber, had written a comedy called *Is Zat So?*, about a prizefighter and his manager who are suddenly thrust into New York society. The premise was not exactly an original one, but the script had an unusual freshness and vitality, and it looked like a promising possibility for the 1924–1925 Broadway season. The problem lay in the fact that Gleason and Taber, who were producing the show, had run out of money. Like many other novice producers, they approached Lee for financial help. He liked the script and advanced the pair enough to bring *Is Zat So?* to Broadway in January 1925.

Flyer for James Gleason and Richard Taber's Is Zat So? *(1925). Critics agreed that* Is Zat So? *was an engaging play— among them Lee and J.J.'s particular nemesis, Alexander Woollcott. Woollcott called* Is Zat So? *a "homely, original, unpretentious, immensely enjoyable comedy," and "a heart warming success." But he did manage a modest dig at Shubert shrewdness in his review. The show's impoverished authors, he said, were desperate for backing, and "had been promised a hearing from Lee Shubert. The hour was appointed, the actors gathered. But there was no Mr. Shubert. Two hours passed and no Mr. Shubert. And then, dropping in like a passerby, came George B. McClellan, a Shubert ally." McClellan, Woollcott said, apologized profusely, magnanimously agreed to watch the performance, and "with the final scene, was ready to talk business."*

For his trouble, Lee acquired not only a substantial piece of the show, which became an instant success, but an option on Gleason's next play, *The Fall Guy*. Gleason's new play, written with producer George Abbott, was a genial comedy about a blue-collar family which inadvertently gets involved with bootleggers. *The Fall Guy*, which opened on Broadway in March of 1925, was an even greater success than *Is Zat So?*, and made satisfying amounts of money for everyone concerned. Gleason, however, ran through most of his share and shortly gave up playwriting and moved to Hollywood, where he built a long and distinguished career as a character actor.

All in all, the first half of the twenties had been a boom period for the Shuberts. Following Sam's tradition, Lee and J.J. continued to work tirelessly to build the company. Fourteen-hour days were common for both, each of whom had taken to handling particular aspects of the business. Although their spheres often overlapped, J.J. was responsible for musicals and for construction and maintenance of theatres. Lee tended to handle straight plays, finances, publicity and advertising, and maintenance of their non-theatrical real estate. Each had his own staff—"Lee's Side" and "J.J.'s Side," as people in the company called them—and the two had fallen into a kind of uneasy truce since the death of their mother, who had been responsible for keeping their stormy relationship more or less under control. Indeed, the brothers had even gone so far as to buy a suburban estate together where they and their sisters' families spent what were probably less than totally restful summers.

By the mid-twenties, Lee and J.J.'s pre-eminence had led them into endlessly complicated business situations. Among them was an abortive lawsuit for half a million dollars, brought by the Vaudeville Actors Guild, and a protracted three-way negotiation involving Actors' Equity, the Producers Association, and the Shuberts. Lee and J.J. resigned in a huff from the Association and sought to make their own private arrangements with Equity, which was seeking a new agreement with Broadway producers. "Getting your own way," as John would later write, "was almost a registered trademark of the Shubert family." Lee and J.J. now had theirs; they were both independents and the most powerful figures in American show business. The situation offered interesting opportunities.

In 1924 the Shuberts began to issue stock in their company. Their report to stockholders two years later indicated that they owned more than 90 theatres across the country and booked some 750 others. By December of 1927, they had added three more houses and their stock stood at a record high. As the twenties advanced, they expanded overseas, as well as in North America, with leases on five London theatres, together with Vienna's *Theatre an der Wein*. In fact, as would become apparent at the end of the decade, they had overextended. The road had been gradually declining throughout the teens and twenties, and by 1925 the number of operating legitimate theatres across the country was down more than 50 percent from 1910. The growth of the movies, higher transportation costs, the Federal amusement tax that began during the war years, and an oversupply of houses built as a result of the Open Door Policy, were slowly leading the American theatre away from its years of immense prosperity. Yet, as Lee once put it, "there was so much money we all lost our balance a bit."

By the second half of the twenties the operetta craze was actually on its way out, but the Shuberts—or J.J., at any rate—remained convinced of the eternal appeal of the form, even in the case of such lukewarm examples as *Princess Flavia*. The show, which opened at the Century in the fall of 1925, was a musical version of Anthony Hope's famous novel *The Prisoner of Zenda*. Several years earlier an adaptation of the novel had had a successful run as a straight play. The new version was the work of two Shubert veterans—Romberg and Harry B. Smith—and was, in many ways, reminiscent of Romberg and Dorothy Donnelly's *The Student Prince*, but without that show's vitality. It did feature, however, two important singers, Harry Welchman and Evelyn Herbert, and an impressive male chorus similar to the one from the earlier Romberg-Donnelly show.

The well-worn plot involves an Englishman, Rudolf Rassendyl, who is a virtual double for the Crown Prince of Ruritania. When the real prince is unable to appear at his coronation as king of the tiny nation, Rassendyl agrees to impersonate him. The Prince's cousin, Princess Flavia, is taken in by the deception and falls in love with the bogus Prince. Eventually, Rassendyl reveals the truth to Princess

Sheet music cover for "Convent Bells Are Ringing" from Princess Flavia (1925). The show was written by two Shubert staff members, Romberg and Smith, and directed by a third, J.C. Huffman. By no means all of Lee and J.J.'s shows were staged by staff, but throughout their producing careers they employed a number of staff directors and choreographers. Because J.J. was a frustrated director, their lot was not always a happy one. Fred Allen recalled an incident when Huffman begged J.J. not to open a new show without a dress rehearsal. But the opening was sold out and J.J. was having none of it. "The curtain rang up at 8:30," Allen said, "and came down for the end of the first act at 1:30 A.M. . . . the whole night was a colorful nightmare."

Flavia, the two part company, and Flavia is reunited with the real ruler. The show had a five-month run in New York and toured with reasonable success. But *Princess Flavia* was clearly a minor example of Romberg's work.

The next year, J.J. presented, with considerably more success, another Ruritanian musical, *Countess Maritza*, starring the actress-violinist Odette Myrtil and Walter Woolf, the singer who had appeared for the Shuberts in *The Dream Girl*. The now-forgotten *Countess Maritza* opened at the Shubert and ran for more than 300 performances during the 1926–1927 season. The music was by Emmerich Kalman, who, with Romberg, had created one of J.J.'s favorite shows, *Her Soldier Boy*. The book was the product of the ubiquitous Harry B. Smith—his 115th Broadway show—and Alfred Grunwald. There were musical interpolations by Romberg and Al Goodman, later a well-known orchestra leader.

Harry K. Morton, Odette Myrtil, and Carl Randall in Countess Maritza
(1926); and Myrtil and Walter Woolf in the same show. Like Countess Maritza *itself, Woolf and Myrtil, are long forgotten. But at the time both were
important names in musical theatre—and especially in operetta. The violin-
playing Myrtil got her start with Ziegfeld and had considerable success as an
entertainer in Europe before returning to Broadway. In later years she would
appear in the Shubert's fictionalized biography of Chopin,* White Lilacs, *and
in Jerome Kern and Otto Harbach's great success* The Cat and the Fiddle.
*Woolf was a major star who was seen in such well-known shows as Lee and
J.J.'s* Florodora *revival, Oscar Straus's* The Last Waltz, The Passing Show,
and Victor Herbert's The Dream Girl.

The rather convoluted story takes place in an unnamed Balkan state
bordering Hungary and involves handsome Count Tassilo Endrody,
who sells the family estates to cover his father's debts. Count Tassilo
goes to work incognito as an overseer for the extremely wealthy
Countess Maritza in order to provide a dowry for his sister, Countess
Lisa. To escape her suitors, Maritza has declared her love for an
imaginary nobleman, Baron Koloman Szupan. The real Szupan turns
up to claim her, but soon falls in love with Lisa. Maritza and Tassilo
have a falling out, and he is urged to leave the Countess's castle by
Manja, the young gypsy girl who loves him. In the end, however, the
Count's rich aunt, Princess Bozena Klopensheim, restores her
nephew's estate to him and convinces Countess Maritza to confess
her love for the young nobleman. The show spawned the extremely
popular "Play, Gypsies—Dance, Gypsies," which was sung by
Woolf as the impoverished Count.

By the twenties, Harry B. Smith was the Shubert house librettest
supreme. In addition to *Countess Maritza* and *Princess Flavia,* he
would turn out more than a half a dozen Shubert shows with Romberg, Emmerich Kalman, and others. Among them were *Springtime
for Youth* (1922), *Caroline* (1923), *Naughty Riquette* (designed as a
vehicle for Mitzi Hajos, 1926), *The Circus Princess* (1927), *Cherry
Blossoms* (1927), and *The Red Robe* (yet another Walter Woolf epic,
1928). In their continual search for another *Blossom Time,* Lee and
J.J. had set Smith to the task of reworking a Hungarian libretto for

The Love Song (1925), a show about a love affair between composer Jacques Offenbach and the Empress Eugenie. As a somewhat jaded Smith pointed out in his autobiography, *First Nights and First Editions,* "the reading of numerous memoirs failed to disclose even the mildest flirtation between Offenbach and Eugenie." What is more, Smith wrote, Offenbach was "an eccentric-looking little man" with mutton-chop whiskers, whose appearance was "comic rather than romantic." Nonetheless, "to avoid biographical accuracy, the role of the creator of the cancan was assigned to a good-looking young tenor."

The Love Song was no *Blossom Time,* but it did manage a six-month run. In the stories-of-great-composers vein, Smith also created the libretto for *White Lilacs* in 1928. The show, which managed eighteen weeks, was yet another *Blossom Time* knock-off, this one a biography of Chopin, with George Sand played by Odette Myrtil, complete with violin, and oldtime comedian De Wolf Hopper doing the comedy business.

In January of 1926, perhaps encouraged by the success of the first edition of *Gay Paree,* Lee and J.J. would try out another Harold

Costume by Ernest Schrapps for The Love Song, *1925, a musical biography of Jacques Offenbach which incorporated a number of his melodies. Schrapps, who created costumes for more than a dozen Shubert shows, including* The Passing Show, Artists and Models, *and* Princess Flavia, *was for some years the head designer at the famous Broadway costume house, the Brooks Costume Company. The settings for* The Love Song *were by Lee and J.J.'s chief scene designer at the time, Watson Barratt. Barratt, who began his career as a magazine illustrator, had begun working for the Shuberts in 1918, on Jolson's* Sinbad.

"Cleopatra's Barge" scene from the second edition of the Shubert revue A
Night in Paris *(1926). The show was one of the many minor revues that Lee
and J.J. ground out to take advantage of a currently popular theme or a group
of performers whose material they liked and who were available at the right
moment—and at the right price. Musical theatre historian Gerald Bordman
points out that* A Night in Paris *was filled with "bright low-paid youngsters
on the way up," and that "the evening had the empty glitter of so many
Shubert assemblages." But the show was successful, and Bordman adds that
"the Shuberts knew what the public wanted, at least that not unsizable
section of the public they considered theirs."*

Atteridge revue with vaguely French overtones, *A Night in Paris*. The
popular girlie show, which ran for almost 200 performances at the
Casino de Paris, the Shubert cabaret in the Winter Garden theatre,
featured, among others, comedian Jack Pearl and the Gertrude
Hoffman Dancers, dressed as Zulu warriors and as various denominations of currency. The "A Night in . . ." premise was a workable if

not precisely innovative framing device for a leg show, and Lee and J.J. would use it several more times in later years, with varying degrees of success.

By the second half of the twenties, J.J. may well have felt that Sigmund Romberg, his personal discovery, was also his personal property. But the composer had other ideas. A number of J.J.'s best staff writers, composers, and directors were starting to leave him for other managements, and the quality of his musical productions was dropping noticeably. Among the defectors was Romberg, who, in 1926, joined with Otto Harbach and Oscar Hammerstein to present the fabulously successful *The Desert Song.* Two years later, Romberg would work with Hammerstein again on another huge success, *The New Moon.* Predictably, J.J. was hurt and angry at the defection.

Over the years Romberg had presented the Shuberts with some of their most prestigious and profitable musicals and revues, among them *Blossom Time, Maytime,* and *The Student Prince,* as well as several editions of the *Passing Show* and various Jolson vehicles. Now Romberg was gaining his independence. But between the two rival shows, J.J. did manage to snare him for a new project. Once again, in 1927, Romberg was teamed with Dorothy Donnelly, with whom he had worked on both *Blossom Time* and *The Student Prince.* Their new collaboration, *My Maryland,* was a more than respectable hit, with a New York run of more than 300 performances. The show featured soprano Evelyn Herbert in the leading role, as well as yet another large male chorus.

The Romberg-Donnelly musical was an adaptation of *Barbara Frietchie,* an 1899 play by Clyde Fitch. (The Fitch play, in turn, had been based on a famous incident during the Civil War which also inspired the popular poem by John Greenleaf Whittier.) In the musical a Union officer, Captain Trumbull, falls in love with Barbara Frietchie, who is not the elderly woman of the Whittier poem, but a young Maryland belle. Her father forbids the marriage, and Barbara and Trumbull elope. Before the ceremony can take place, however, he is called away to battle. Shortly, Trumbull is brought back gravely wounded to the Frietchie house, where Mr. Frietchie orders him out. But Barbara pleads for the wounded officer's life and her father finally relents and allows him to stay. At the show's climax—which is

The Confederate Soldiers chorus from My Maryland, *1927. Although it was never as popular as* Blossom Time *or* The Student Prince, My Maryland *would become a favorite with summer stock companies, schools, and amateur theatres. The rental files on the show contain dozens of programs from such groups as the Montclair Operetta Club, the Wilmington Drama League, the San Antonio Civic Opera Company, St. John Terrell's Music Circus, and the Sacred Heart High School in an unnamed New Jersey community. The last performance recorded in the files took place in 1976 in Indiana as a Bicentennial project. For many years producers could obtain virtually everything necessary to present the show, including sets and costumes, from Lee and J.J.'s Century Library and its subsidiaries.*

loosely based on the Civil War incident—Barbara hangs a United States flag from a window of her father's house just as Confederate General Stonewall Jackson and his troops are passing by. Jackson admires the young woman's courage, declines to execute the Union officer, and places Barbara and Trumbull under his own special protection. The reviews of *My Maryland* were somewhat mixed, but the audience response was excellent and one song from the show, "Your Land and My Land," was to become a patriotic standard.

Although it had an American setting, *My Maryland* was basically a conventional European operetta of the sort that had long been the centerpiece of Shubert producing. And in spite of the show's success, it was now becoming obvious that an important new approach to musical theatre was rising to challenge Lee and J.J.'s traditional tastes. On December 27, 1927, the Shubert's arch rival Florenz Ziegfeld opened a Jerome Kern–Oscar Hammerstein musical. *Show Boat,* unlike *My Maryland,* was a musical *play,* with the songs carefully and credibly integrated into the action. Soon this new brand of musical would reshape America's theatrical history; but Lee and J.J. never seemed totally at home with it. In fact, they would cling stubbornly to the florid and often incomprehensible operetta form for years to come.

In September of 1929, for example, Lee and J.J. would launch a series of popular-priced revivals of traditional musical shows. They were mounted cheaply at the Jolson, for short runs, using scenery and costumes from the Shubert warehouses. For reasons not altogether clear, the Shuberts kept a low profile, operating as the Jolson Theatre Musical Comedy Company. The series began as a Victor Herbert festival, and half a dozen of his shows were included, starting with a revival of *Sweethearts* in September, and moving on through such classic Herbert works as *Mlle. Modiste,* with the oldtime star Fritzi Scheff, and *Naughty Marietta,* starring Ilse Marvenga, who had gained an immense following in *The Student Prince.* The premise was so successful that Lee and J.J. added operettas by other composers, for a total of eleven shows. Several of them toured, and there were plans to continue and expand the series for the 1930–1931 season. The plans never came to fruition, probably because of the Depression, but the premise of operetta at popular prices was one that the

Shuberts would return to several times during the thirties and forties—long after the form had passed its prime.

As early as the middle of the decade there had been strong indications
that the show business which the Shuberts had known and helped to
create was changing. The Broadway season of 1925–1926 witnessed
more than twice as many shows in twice as many theatres as a decade
before. But, as inexperienced producers and theatre owners entered
the obviously lucrative field, the number of failures increased substantially, and the total number of weeks actually played by shows
began to decline. In 1925, almost three-quarters of the productions
on Broadway failed to make money. Yet, in a sense, the boom continued; a record 264 shows opened during the 1927–1928 season.
From that point on, however, the number of shows would decline,
along with weeks played. The causes were the overbuilding of theatres, too many poor plays and amateurish productions, the rapidly
rising cost of producing, inefficient ticket distribution, the constant
decline of the road since the teens, and the competition from vaudeville, radio, and especially the new talking films. The stock market
crash would shortly add the finishing touch.

Still, the late twenties was a time of immense prosperity for the
Shuberts. As A.J. Liebling phrased it in the *New Yorker:* "By 1927
there weren't so many companies of 'The Student Prince' and
'Blossom Time' as there once had been, but five road companies of
'My Maryland' had joined the survivors and the nation was filled
with song. The coffers of the Shubert Theatre Corporation were
filled with cash." Lee and J.J. were producing widely and still building theatres, both out of town and in New York City. By now the
Shubert real estate holdings in New York had become little short of
monumental. Among other parcels of land in the city, they owned or
leased virtually everything on Forty-fourth and Forty-fifth streets,
between Broadway and Eighth Avenue, with the exception of two
hotel sites. On the eve of the Depression, Lee and J.J. had control of
what was almost certainly the single most valuable parcel of theatrical
real estate in the world.

Recent additions to their collection of theatres included the Majestic, a large musical house, on Forty-fourth Street, and the smaller

Portrait of Ethel Barrymore from a souvenir program; and a photograph of the theatre bearing her name as it appeared in 1972. The Barrymore, opened in 1928, on the eve of the Depression, was the last theatre the Shuberts would build on Broadway. By 1957, J.J. was considering the possibility of entering into a partnership to run the house. He addressed the issue in a letter to his son John with his usual candor—and a touch of weariness: "You are asking me a very peculiar question: would I let Huntington Hartford become a partner with us in the operation of the Barrymore Theatre? By all means, yes. . . . I would not lose the opportunity of doing something with Mr. Hartford regarding the Barrymore Theatre, and anything else he wants to come in on. I think we should try to make our lot much easier."

Royale and Theatre Masque (later renamed for the producer John Golden), a block to the north. All three buildings were erected in 1927 as real estate investments by the Chanin brothers, owners of a construction company, and were designed by theatre architect Herbert Krapp.

The Shuberts' newest theatre in New York was Krapp's Ethel Barrymore on West Forty-seventh Street, just a few blocks from the center of Lee and J.J.'s activities. In the by now long-established Broadway tradition, Barrymore was given a theatre bearing her name when she signed with the Shuberts in 1928. The theatre opened in December of that year, with its namesake starring in *The Kingdom of God*, a forgettable religious drama by the popular Spanish playwright G. Martinez Sierra, who is probably best remembered in America today, if at all, for his earlier play *The Cradle Song*. *The Kingdom of God*, which was directed by Barrymore herself under the pseudonym E.M. Blythe, was an unabashed vehicle for its star as the nun Sister Gracia. The response was good and the show managed a run of almost 100 performances during the 1928–1929 season.

Also appearing at the Ethel Barrymore soon after its opening was a successful comedy, *Bird in Hand*, by the English poet and playwright John Drinkwater, which Lee moved into the new theatre from the Morosco, as well as a hit drama called *Death Takes a Holiday*, an Italian play by Alberto Cassella, adapted by Walter Ferris, which ran for eight months, beginning late in December of 1929. The show toured twice and later returned to New York for a second Broadway run in 1931. In the play, Death (popular actor Philip Merivale) assumes human form and goes on vacation disguised as a nobleman. At a country estate he falls in love with Grazia (Rose Hobart), the daughter of the owner. She reciprocates his love and willingly joins him as he returns to his kingdom on "the other side." In a pre-Broadway tour Grazia's role had been played by Katharine Hepburn, who received terrible notices and was replaced by Hobart before the New York opening.

J.J. was plunging ahead with musicals, among them *Boom Boom*, a show based on a French original, starring Jeanette MacDonald, with comedian Frank McIntyre as the aging playboy to whom she is—as the Shubert play catalogue delicately put it—"married but not

Sample advertisements from a press book for Bird in Hand, 1929. In addition to a selection of ads for use by theatre managers, the press book contains information about available posters, flyers, and photographs for Bird in Hand, as well as a selection of press releases about the show which could be used by columnists and entertainment editors in need of ready-made copy. Among the subjects addressed by the releases are the problems involved with meals served on stage during the show ("When Nicholas Joy, the pompous lawyer, asks for white wine, he gets plain water. His sherry is sparkling water.") and off-stage sound effects ("Rain is made by the use of several pounds of small shot inside a revolving drum, the circumference of which is enclosed by wire screening.").

Flyer for Death Takes a Holiday, 1929. Its star, Philip Merivale, was generally praised for his work, and the play had a good run. As the quote from William Lyon Phelps of Yale suggests, the Shubert press department marketed Death Takes a Holiday as something of a high-brow dramatic event. But not all of the reviewers agreed with that judgment, especially the higher brows among the critical establishment. Gilbert Seldes compared it to old-fashioned plays "in which the mysterious stranger turns out to be the Great God Pan or the Light of the East." John Mason Brown was reminded of "one of those allegories you used to take part in in Sunday school, except for the fact that you are no longer in it and Philip Merivale is."

Sheet music for "Shake High, Shake Low," from Boom Boom, *1929. The show starred hefty comedian Frank McIntyre as a kind of Daddy Browning satyr, and Jeanette MacDonald, whom critic Percy Hammond described in his review of the show as "a fair, shapely and musical soprano."* Prior to their performances in Boom Boom, *MacDonald and another cast member, Archie Leach, soon to be Cary Grant, had been called for screen tests by Paramount. MacDonald soon moved on to Hollywood eventually becoming a partner for Nelson Eddy; Leach remained in New York for several more years, appearing as Max in* A Wonderful Night, *Lee and J.J.'s elaborately staged 1929 version of* Die Fledermaus.

mated." *Boom Boom,* which opened at the Casino in January 1929 to less than ecstatic reviews and a run of 72 performances, had Lee's constant companion Marcella Swanson in a small role, as well as a handsome young actor named Archie Leach, later known as Cary Grant. More successful was J.J.'s summer revue *A Night in Venice,* which ran for 175 performances at the Shubert, starting in May of 1929. The dances were staged by the as yet relatively unknown Busby Berkeley, who in February had choreographed another of J.J.'s revues, *Pleasure Bound.*

Pleasure Bound was a retread version with music of Charles Klein's 1913 farce *Potash and Perlmutter.* The new show went through a number of incarnations before it finally arrived on Broadway, and the

The Dodge Twins in A Night in Venice, *1929. The Dodge Twins did one of the "sister acts" popular during the twenties (the most famous was probably the Dolly Sisters, an act that had appeared in several Shubert shows, including* Greenwich Village Follies *of 1924). The show in which the Dodges performed was loud, rambunctious, vulgar, and highly successful. "'A Night in Venice,'" Brooks Atkinson wrote, "spares no energy to entertain the trade. Among the more noticeable of its physical antics are one kick in the mouth, a smarting succession of slaps on the face, a yank of the nose, a bear-wrestling number, the dropping of one person smack into the orchestra pit, not to enumerate the endless pushing and shoving involved in [Ted] Healey's dominance of the book." Healey was a knockabout vaudeville and film comic, from whose act the legendary Three Stooges would emerge.*

Press office flyer showing the revolving stage used in the 1929 Shubert adaptation of Johann Strauss's Die Fledermaus, A Wonderful Night. *The Shuberts got considerable mileage out of the scenic concept, which was something of a novelty in the United States at the time. A Wonderful Night was a reasonable success, considering that the country was entering a period of financial panic, and it even drew a somewhat backhanded rave from an old adversary, critic George Jean Nathan. "The Shubert firm," Nathan said, "has given the operetta the title, 'A Wonderful Night.' It is a rotten title, but it is excellent criticism, at least in a musical direction. The Majestic Theatre has become a sanatorium for all ears sickened by the yah-yah-yah, hey-hey-hey din that passes for music on most stages to the right and left of it."*

result contained only shreds of Klein's original plot. It did, however, retain the two title characters, a pair of comic refugees from the dress business, now renamed Pfeiffer and Fisher. Playing the eccentric pair, who amble from their shop to roadhouses on Long Island and "futuristic hotels in Florida," were comic Jack Pearl and accordionist and comedian Phil Baker. The chaotic show led to generally poor reviews and a rift between Pearl and J.J., who had been close associates for many years.

The young Archie Leach was to reappear in a more popular Shubert production, *A Wonderful Night,* which opened at the end of October 1929, and managed a run of fifteen weeks. (*A Wonderful Night* was one of several Shubert reworkings over the years of Johann Strauss's *Die Fledermaus,* among them a curious 1912 Shubert version called *The Merry Countess,* which featured the Dolly Sisters, a popular song and dance team.) Leach was a somewhat dubious choice for *A Wonderful Night* since he was not a singer. But posed in front of the now ubiquitous male chorus, he looked the part of Max (the Eisenstein role in *Die Fledermaus*), and the show proved to be an important stepping stone in Leach's career.

A Wonderful Night turned out to be something of a burden for Lee and J.J., who, as a result of the show, became involved in a welter of lawsuits with the Strauss estate and with the important Viennese director Max Reinhardt, who claimed that the Shuberts had pirated his staging of the show. But that was to be the least of their troubles. *A Wonderful Night* had opened almost in tandem with the stock-market crash, and shortly the Broadway theatre establishment, with Lee and J.J. at its center, was in total financial disarray.

V
CRASH

The Shuberts discovered, like the Theatre Guild, that the only way to beat the Depression along Broadway was to keep producing shows.

JOHN SHUBERT

In the months after the stock market crash, Lee and J.J. resolutely continued to produce, in several cases with reasonable success. But the lines at their box offices were becoming shorter by the day as around the country money for non-essentials disappeared. They did well, however, with several straight plays. Their *Topaze* was a charming comedy by the French playwright Marcel Pagnol about a schoolmaster who is exploited by crooks and who ultimately turns the tables on them by employing their own methods. *Topaze,* which opened at the Music Box in February 1930, with Frank Morgan as the simple teacher, managed a run of twenty weeks in New York and twenty-five weeks on the road, in spite of increasingly hard times. In January 1931, Lee also successfully presented the Pirandello classic, *As You Desire Me,* with Judith Anderson, which ran for some four months at the Maxine Elliott.

Also fairly successful was Romberg's latest musical for the Shuberts, *Nina Rosa,* which appeared at the Majestic in September 1930. Working with Romberg on the show were two other talented figures from the musical theatre world, Otto Harbach and Irving Caesar. The book was by Harbach (born Otto Hauerbach), the son of a Danish immigrant family, who came to New York in 1901 to study at

Frank Morgan, as a French schoolmaster, and his class, from Topaze, *1930. The child actors in the company received considerable attention in the press, which was bombarded by releases about the boys and their backgrounds. The culminating publicity stunt involved another Shubert show,* Bird in Hand, *the successful John Drinkwater comedy. In celebration of the first anniversary of* Bird in Hand, *boy actors from* Topaze *were cast in Drinkwater's play for a single Saturday morning performance. The stunt worked admirably. The critics were charmed by the performance, which Whitney Bolton of the* Morning Telegraph *said, "had a touching quality, a bland freshness that was cool and charming and enormously fetching."*

Judith Anderson in Pirandello's As You Desire Me, *1931; and Watson Barratt's set for the play. Lee's show had a fair run, in spite of respectful but distinctly unenthusiastic reviews from virtually every daily critic. Gilbert Gabriel called it a "glum play in a thick fog," and Brooks Atkinson pointed out that "Pirandello cannot make plays of undramatic phantoms." Burns Mantle could only point to "a last act that, thanks mainly to Judith Anderson's splendid performance in the role of the heroine, creates briefly a definite and stirring interest." It was clearly Anderson's remarkable performance that brought in audiences.* As You Desire Me *was precisely the sort of self-consciously arty straight play that infuriated J.J., who would later complain to his son John about Lee's productions of "lousy dramatic shows which nobody else wanted and nobody cared about."*

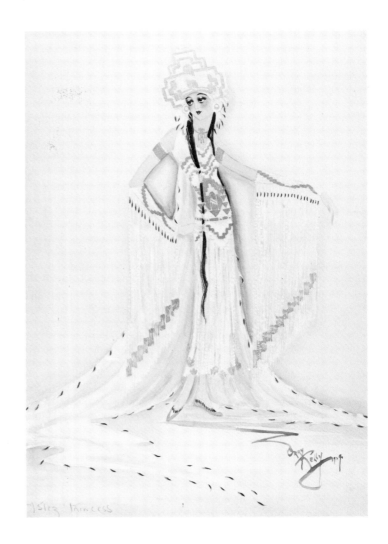

Scene design by Watson Barratt for Act II, scene 1 of Nina Rosa, *1930; Barratt's scheme for a stage curtain for the show "in old Peruvian style"; and a "Peruvian Indian" costume design by well-known Broadway costumer Orry Kelly. In a release for the show headed "Peruvian Stuff," the Shubert press department offered drama editors around the country a scholarly aside: "Permission from the [Peruvian] government had to be obtained in order to perform the famous ceremonial dance outside of the mountain temples in which it has been a feature ever since the inception of the Inca theory of religion. Students of Inca lore have been attending 'Nina Rosa' in ever increasing numbers, finding material there that it would, ordinarily, have taken a trip to Cuzco for them to get."*

Columbia University. Harbach had become a major librettist and lyricist, with credits on such important shows as *The Firefly* (1912), *Rose Marie* (1924), and *No! No! Nanette!* (1925). Caesar, who wrote the lyrics for *Nina Rosa,* was also a Broadway veteran, whose "Swanee," written with George Gershwin, and "My Mammy" had been turned into instant hits by Jolson in the Shuberts' *Sinbad* of 1918.

Nina Rosa featured Ethelind Terry, who had starred in Ziegfeld's sensational *Rio Rita* three years earlier. *Rio Rita* had run for almost 500 performances; the Shuberts' *Nina Rosa* managed only 137, but received respectable reviews and, considering the growing hard times, sold reasonably well. Like *Rio Rita,* the new show was a frontier odyssey. Set in and around Cuzco, Peru, the story centers on a young woman, Nina Rosa, who has been cheated out of her gold mine by Don Fernando, a rich Argentinian. She is in love with an American mining engineer, Jack Haines, who supports her claim.

When it is discovered that the mine is a potential bonanza, Don Fernando hatches a plot to murder Jack. The assassin is to be Pablo, the son of Nina Rosa's old nurse and now Don Fernando's head gaucho. The lovers flee to the mine and, in the show's climactic moments, enter a sacred golden chamber where the local Indians are performing an ancient ritual. They are followed by Pablo and his gauchos, who abduct Nina Rosa and wall up Jack in the ritual chamber. Jack escapes, Nina Rosa is saved, her claim to the mine is found valid, and Jack welcomes as his bride the richest woman in Peru.

Nina Rosa was to be the Shuberts' most successful show for some time to come. New plays were closing quickly, and Lee and J.J., like a number of producers, were cutting ticket prices in a desperate attempt to attract audiences. They tried every conceivable ploy. During 1931, for example, the Shuberts staged low-priced revivals of *Blossom Time* and *The Student Prince* at the Ambassador and the Majestic. Both shows were nothing more than the road companies of the two hits, which had been touring endlessly outside New York, and neither featured a name performer. Lee and J.J., however, did try to fill houses with their greatest name, Al Jolson, whom they brought back from Hollywood to star in a German import, *The Wonder Bar.*

The Wonder Bar was adapted by Irving Caesar and Aben Kandel and starred Jolson, now in whiteface, as Monsieur Al, the proprietor of a Paris cabaret. Assisting him were some important performers, including Patsy Kelly and Arthur Treacher. For the event, the small Nora Bayes theatre on top of the Shuberts' Forty-fourth Street Theatre was converted into the French nightclub, and Jolson was featured in a number of fairly unmemorable songs. Most were by Robert Katscher, who had composed the original score, although Jolson interpolated a few numbers, among them a French version of "My Mammy." The show, which opened to reasonably good reviews, managed a scant ten-week run as the Depression increased in intensity. Jolson, bored and uncomfortable in his role, headed back to Hollywood to work on a new film.

During the early years of the Depression, Lee and J.J. were in a far stronger position than smaller, financially less secure producers and theatre owners. Even so, they found it increasingly necessary to pare down unprofitable theatre holdings and to cut back substantially on their producing activities. During 1932 they disposed of their London theatres and closed down the Shubert in New Haven. And throughout 1932 and 1933 they produced fewer than a dozen shows, only a fraction of the number they mounted each year during the late twenties. But Lee and J.J. were not yet in such financial difficulty that they could resist a bargain. In 1932 they picked up the Chanin brothers Forty-sixth Street Theatre at a discount price; and Lee, at a bankruptcy sale, managed to buy the rights to all of the works produced by the late Arthur Hammerstein for only $700. Included were such valuable shows as *The Firefly* (1921), by Rudolph Friml and Otto Harbach, and *Rose Marie* (1924), with music by Friml and Herbert Stothart and book and lyrics by Harbach and Oscar Hammerstein II. The Shuberts managed to sell the motion picture rights to *The Firefly* for a considerable profit, and later featured both shows in their play rental catalogue.

By the Depression, Lee and J.J. had become distinctly middle-aged and clearly less than beloved by most of the Broadway community. J.J.'s crudity and his explosive temper, and Lee's intimidating reserve—together with their obvious lack of sophistication and their uncanny talent for making money where others could not—had made them a pair to be viewed with a mixture of fear and affection. To much of the press and the theatrical world they had become a kind of old-fashioned but slightly sinister comedy turn.

A.J. Liebling would describe Lee in 1939 as "a short man whose appearance is so ostentatiously youthful that he is usually suspected of being very old. His face is a deep copper red all year round, a result of the sun-ray treatments and sun baths which he takes whenever he gets a chance . . . his upturned eyebrows and the deep wrinkles at the corners of his eyes make him look something like a good-natured Indian—Willie Howard, perhaps, in war chief makeup . . . Mr.

Lee's voice has an indefinable foreign accent; he is always polite, tentatively friendly, and on guard."

Humorist Corey Ford, who was co-author of *Hold Your Horses,* an unsuccessful show produced by the Shuberts in 1933, would recall J.J. as a kind of Damon Runyon Broadway character. In his book *The Time of Laughter,* Ford recorded his first impressions of J.J. during the thirties. "He was squat and dumpy, and sagged at the belly," Ford said. "His short little body was as broad in the buttocks as a ferryboat, but from the waist it tapered upward toward his narrow hunched shoulders, giving him the general shape of an egg. His white-maned head rode well down on the front slope of the egg, and his face was flat-nosed and Mongolian. He shuffled a little as he stepped forward from his desk to greet us, his hands in his pocket, his head thrust forward and wagging from side to side, like a mud turtle walking perpendicularly on the end of its shell." Although Ford was later to fulminate about J.J.'s interference with *Hold Your Horses,* he was initially reassured by what he saw as a kind of Goldwynesque charm: "'I want to do something worthwhile in the theatre, boys,' he told us with a catch in his voice, 'something I can look back on when I'm dead. Your little play here is a work of art. Such wit! Such spontanuity!'"

The result of such encounters was a cornucopia of Broadway "Shubert jokes." In a typical—and printable—one, Tallulah Bankhead, who appeared in a number of Shubert shows, introduces a friend to Lee and J.J. "Dah-ling," she says, "I want you to meet the Shubert brothers—S.H. and I.T." Lee and J.J. were obviously aware of their black comedy reputation—it was certainly no secret and now seemed to be approaching an almost mythological level. J.J. did little about it; Lee, more and more, threw himself into committee work and charitable activities. As always, he obviously felt a strong need to make the kind of formal gestures that would produce respect and affection. But, as always, he seemed not to know just how.

Yet both Lee and J.J. demonstrated a kind of disarming generosity to the people with whom they had worked over the years. In fact, although the Shuberts were famous as tight-fisted producers and managers, both had long been well known for their personal handouts

J.J. Shubert in Egypt about 1936. J.J. was widely regarded as having no discernible sense of humor—except in comparison with his brother Lee. Yet the photograph somehow manages to catch a hint of bizarre comedy, as does his response to a young actress who wrote to him in 1945, inquiring about the quality of a Shubert road company with which she was planning to sign a contract. She asked what shows J.J. would present, who his conductor was, and who the leading man and the director would be. J.J. replied that "you evidently forgot to ask me what I have for breakfast. I think I will advise you. Sometimes I have coffee and sometimes tea. I start off with a little grapefruit, when it is in season, or orange juice, and toast. That is all. I never ask for the chef's name."

to hard-pressed actors, stagehands, and musicians. Kathryn Lynch, who spent thirty-eight years with the company, most of them on "J.J.'s Side," as manager of the Century Library, the company's play-leasing operation, recalled in an interview that she had "often witnessed Shubert generosity to employees in financial difficulties and to show girls having a hard time finding work. Mitzi Hajos [a former Shubert star] was given a job with 'Ma' Simmons, the casting director for many years. The Shuberts took care of Simmons himself until he died in a nice retirement home with every wish of his fulfilled. There are many more examples."

During the Depression, in the face of plummeting box-office receipts at Shubert theatres, Lee and J.J. drastically increased their handout lists, kept many of their old employees on the payroll when there was little for them to do, and bailed out a number of small producers whose shows were in financial trouble. Sometimes the Shuberts even turned a profit on their philanthropy, as in the case of their old partner William Brady's 1929 production of Elmer Rice's *Street Scene*. Brady had picked up the rights to Rice's controversial play about slum life for $6000 after it had been turned down by countless other producers. In the middle of rehearsals Brady ran out of money and appealed to Lee for help. Lee bought half the show for a modest sum and *Street Scene* went on to win a Pulitzer Prize and to become one of the few great hits of the Depression era. Ultimately Brady and Lee each made a half-million-dollar profit from the production and another $165,000 from the sale of the motion picture rights.

Prior to the success of *Street Scene*, the Shuberts had preferred to produce on their own; now, in a period in which it was wise to limit the extent of their financial commitments, they became increasingly interested in the possibilities presented by investment in other producers' shows. In the years to come, as they produced less themselves, they would constantly look for attractive investments in other people's plays which they could book into Shubert theatres. Two of their investments during the thirties would prove to be among the most important plays ever associated with the Shubert name: Sidney Kingsley's Pulitzer-Prize winning *Men in White,* a celebrated drama about a young doctor's life in a hospital, produced by the Group

Theatre in 1933, and Lillian Hellman's grim study of the evil quality in ordinary people, *The Children's Hour,* produced in 1934.

As times got worse in the early thirties, the number of operating theatres in New York dropped from seventy-two to thirty-six, and nearly half the theatre workers in the city were out of a job. Lee and J.J. now stopped production on a number of shows and dropped their leases on half a dozen theatres in New York and a number on the road. Most of their other houses were dark and their producing activities had dwindled to a mere handful of shows. Ironically, in 1932, in order to keep the road going, Lee and J.J. were forced to combine with the Erlanger office and a former Syndicate partner, Marcus Heiman, to develop a common booking establishment out of the old Keith's United Booking Office.

At the time of the stock market crash the Shuberts' worth on paper had been $72 million; after the crash they were reduced to assets of less than a million and a half. In 1931 the Shubert Theatrical Corporation went into receivership; two years later, in April of 1933, Lee bought the assets of the company at a bankruptcy auction for a bargain $400,000 in the name of a new corporation, Select Theatres. He was about to start over again.

Meanwhile, during the summer of 1932, Lee and J.J.'s old rival Florenz Ziegfeld had died. The Shubert's view of Ziegfeld was unambiguous. As John phrased it, over the years he had taken on "the appearance of another Erlanger" in the minds of Lee and J.J. For J.J., in particular, Ziegfeld was "dangerous and had to be watched carefully," like "any man who produced a string of hits." Now he was dead, leaving an estate made up of at least half a million dollars in debts. His widow, the actress Billie Burke, was confounded by the financial chaos she had inherited and desperately began to search for some way out. The answer seemed to lie in the *Ziegfeld Follies,* and shortly she appealed to Lee to present a new edition of the famous old revue. Lee liked the idea, and in 1934 he and J.J. would produce the first of several new editions of Ziegfeld's show.

In the meantime, J.J.'s son John had graduated from the University of Pennsylvania and begun work on a law degree at Harvard. By 1933, however, he had left law school and joined his father's staff, where he was to spend a number of uneasy and not altogether happy

J.J. and his son John about 1928. The two were never close, a fact which J.J. clearly came to regret in later years, especially after Lee's death. But he always had difficulty expressing his feelings for his son, except in rather formal and oblique terms connected with business affairs. In 1959, toward the end of his life, for example, he would write to John that "of late we do not see each other to discuss matters that are very important. I know you are busy and I am busy too but our business is of the utmost importance and you should know all about it. We have no one to discuss matters with. It would only take a few minutes a day. We have no one who is interested but ourselves. . . . We are like strangers so I wish you would see me daily and talk things over that might help."

years. Archie Thompson, who was once John's assistant, characterized J.J.'s relationship with his son in an interview. "John was a very, very nice guy. And he was very put upon by his father. His father would say, 'Go ahead, John, do it.' Then J.J. would come along and rip everything apart—really put him down."

Kathryn Lynch phrased it in a different way. She recalled J.J. saying to her that he had left school to go to work in the third grade and had never really had a childhood. "Then he went on. 'My son has a set of trains in his basement. He is a grown man and will be the head of the business some day and he plays with trains.' J.J. did not understand his son, and he was often puzzled, distressed, contemptuous, and worried about the future." As for John himself, Lynch believed that he "felt the pressure and expectations from his father and tried to please him. What he really liked, though, was doing things with his hands. He built boats and did photography. I remember one time when we were together in the darkroom. I was photostating Shubert personal papers and legal documents, and he was developing his negatives. I asked him, "If you could have your druthers, what would you have liked to become? His answer was, 'I would like to be a carpenter.'"

John's initial venture as a co-producer with his father was *Hold Your Horses,* the nostalgic musical about turn-of-the-century New York, with a book by playwright Russel Crouse and Corey Ford, and music and lyrics by a number of relatively obscure composers and lyricists. The show, which opened at the Winter Garden in September of 1933, featured the talented vaudeville comic Joe Cook, who had starred in George M. Cohan's highly successful 1928 musical, *Rain or Shine.* The success was not repeated with *Hold Your Horses,* which J.J. vainly "doctored" at the last minute.

According to Ford, the failure was, in no small part, due to J.J.'s incessant tampering with the show during the rehearsal period. At one rehearsal, Ford suggested in *Time of Laughter,* J.J. made room for more show girls—his sovereign remedy for the ailing musical. "He was in his glory, smirking at the girls, humming to himself, even prancing satyr-like in time with the music," Ford said. "'Give me beauty! I want more beauty!' He draped them voluptuously across steps, around tables, along balconies. He walked them in and out of

Two sketches for show-girl costumes by Russell Patterson for Hold Your Horses, *1933. Brooks Atkinsion of the* New York Times *reluctantly found the show wanting but filled with delightful period touches. Among them were Russell Patterson's "jaunty sets" and "gay costumes of a fabulous era of lacy underthings." Patterson, a Midwesterner who once studied with Monet, had become famous during the twenties as a popularizer of the Flapper image. Although he was primarily an illustrator, cartoonist, and painter, Patterson also designed occasional films and Broadway shows, including portions of Lee and J.J.'s Ziegfeld Follies of 1934. Among the other nostalgic attractions of* Hold Your Horses *were period numbers choreographed by Robert Alton and Harriet Hoctor, two major figures in the dance world who worked on other Shubert shows of the period.*

love scenes, he altered plot scenes to make room for them, he chopped other scenes entirely in which they did not appear. Crouse tried manfully to keep up with the changes, drawing pencil lines through page after page of the script in his lap. I wasn't much help; my mind had gone mercifully numb. All I wanted to do was curl up somewhere and close my eyes and forget. 'I have to think of everything,' I could hear J.J. whining. 'What we lack around here is a dearth of good ideas.' "

Depression audiences seemed uninterested in J.J.'s girls and Joe Cook's old-fashioned vaudeville capers, and the show closed after 88 performances. The failure of *Hold Your Horses* was obviously a blow to John, but at least it brought him his wife, "Eckie," a chorus girl in the show. Kerttu Helene Ecklund, of Finnish extraction, had got her start in the famous Chester Hale shows at the Capitol Theatre, a "presentation house" at which four short live shows were staged throughout the day between the newsreel and the feature film. The

"Eckie" Shubert, John Shubert's wife, whom he met while she was playing in Hold Your Horses. *During the early years of her marriage, Eckie also appeared in small roles in several other Shubert productions, including* The Show Is On *in 1936. Eckie's relationship with the Shubert family was tempestuous: J.J. opposed her marriage to John; although she and John's mother Catherine lived in adjoining houses for many years, they seldom spoke; and her marriage to John, which lasted more than a quarter of a century, was to end with a strange set of circumstances that made newspaper headlines across the country and led to a complex and protracted court case.*

shows in which Eckie appeared were basically vaudeville entertainments made up of conventional variety acts, a star turn, selections by the house orchestra, and numbers by the popular Chester Hale Dancers. (Similar "stage shows" or "prologs" were appearing in many movie theatres during the thirties as vaudeville gradually disappeared from the American scene. John, in fact, had been assigned to work with a brief and unsuccessful Shubert entry into the business, producing tabloid versions of such Shubert properties as *Artists and Models, The Student Prince,* and *The Passing Show* in movie houses.) J.J. was predictably opposed to John's marriage to Eckie, which would take place secretly in the fall of 1937.

The Shuberts' *Ziegfeld Follies,* when it appeared, was a gratifying success. The Shubert–Billie Burke version of the show (with which Burke had little actual connection) was built on a very different model from the original, but it contained some good material and several important Broadway performers, including Fanny Brice, Jane Froman, Eve Arden, and the great vaudeville and revue comics Willie and Eugene Howard. The show, which opened at the Winter Garden in January 1934, was built around music by two relative newcomers to Broadway, composer Vernon Duke and lyricist E.Y. ("Yip") Harburg. The pair provided a pleasant score which included a striking ballad, "Moon About Town," and the popular "What Is There to Say?," both of which were sung by Froman.

Brice performed the first of her soon to be famous "Baby Snooks" sketches, with Howard playing the long-suffering Daddy, and sang a Yiddish-dialect parody of the then famous evangelist Aimee Semple McPherson called "Soul Saving Sadie from Avenue A." Howard also offered what must have been a somewhat bizarre Yiddish version of an interpolated Western song, "The Last Roundup." The song, and another of the show's interpolated Western numbers, "Wagon Wheels," were to become Depression-era standards. All in all, while the show lacked much of the glamour and panache of the Ziegfeld originals, it was well conceived and well produced. And in spite of mixed reviews from critics who looked back nostalgically to the Ziegfeld–Joseph Urban triumphs, the Shuberts' reinterpretation of the *Follies* managed a healthy run of more than 180 performances—almost six months at a time when tickets were very hard to sell.

Design by Albert Johnson for the "Moon About Town" number in the Shubert–Billie Burke-produced Ziegfeld Follies of 1934; and Fanny Brice and Willie Howard in a "Baby Snooks" routine from the same show in which Daddy tells a blasé Snooks the story of George Washington and the cherry tree. Johnson, who would also design Life Begins at 8:40 for Lee and J.J., was only in his early twenties when he worked on the two shows. Brice, a veteran of five previous editions of the Follies under Ziegfeld, was in magnificent form, offering a nudist sketch, a fan-dancer routine, and a classic take-off on evangelist Aimee Semple MacPherson, "Soul Saving Sadie from Avenue A."

Things continued to look up as the new season began. Late in August of 1934 the Shuberts produced what was to be one of their best revues, the long-running *Life Begins at 8:40.* Everything about the show, which opened at the Winter Garden, suggested an extraordinarily high level of quality. *Life Begins at 8:40* starred Bert Lahr, Ray Bolger, comedienne Louella Gear, and singer Frances Williams. The show was composed by Harold Arlen, with lyrics by E. Y. Harburg and Ira Gershwin. The director was John Murray Anderson, the famous revue specialist who had first worked with Lee and J.J. more than a decade before when they produced his *Greenwich Village Follies.*

Life Begins at 8:40 more than lived up to its extraordinary promise. The revue (whose title parodied a popular inspirational book of the day, *Life Begins at Forty*) featured the great comedian Bert Lahr in somewhat more subtle and underplayed comedy than that of his earlier shows. But subtlety was a relative matter with Lahr. In one sketch, "Chin Up," he burlesques the English aristocracy's passionate devotion to family honor in a drawing room that becomes littered with upper-class suicides. In another number, Lahr impersonates a stuffy concert singer who intones a profoundly incoherent art song "written in a little garret on the left bank of Giaconda Canal and . . . entitled 'Things,' simply 'Things.'"

In a second suicide-based routine, "C'est la Vie," Lahr and Bolger meet on a bridge over the Seine, from which both are about to jump because they have been jilted by the same woman, temptress Louella

Life Begins at 8:40 *(1934): advertising flyer for the show; Bert Lahr, Louella Gear, and Ray Bolger; and the Charles Weidman Dancers.* Life Begins at 8:40 *was probably one of Lee and J.J.'s best revues, with an outstanding cast. The Weidman Dancers had previously appeared in the critically acclaimed but not altogether successful revue* Americana *(1932), a show which the Shuberts produced. Charles Weidman, one of the pioneers of modern dance in America, was bringing a new look to Broadway dancing. The fact was not lost on the Shubert press office, which noted in a release that, with the Weidman troupe, "there is gradually coming into being a really new revue dance form. . . . New patterns, new and subtle rhythms and compositions are finding their way into Broadway shows."*

Gear. Gear appears and suggests a ménage-à-trois in the manner of Noel Coward's popular play *Design for Living*. The show also contained an exotic rhumba number, fantastically costumed chorus girls, a revolving stage, and a sprightly song for Bolger and Dixie Dunbar, "You're a Builder-Upper." *Life Beings at 8:40* turned out to be a tonic for Depression-weary audiences and ran for seven months.

The season of 1935–1936 began with *At Home Abroad*, which promised to be a success and in fact managed a six-month run. But like every musical opening that season except the dazzling *On Your Toes*, produced by George Abbott, it failed to make a substantial profit. Billed as "A Musical Holiday from the New York Winter Garden," *At Home Abroad* was a revue-with-a-shred-of-plot, created by the talented young team of composer Arthur Schwartz and lyricist Howard Dietz. It involved a loose bracketing plot about a peripatetic couple named Otis and Henrietta Hatrick who embark on a world tour. Along the way, the Hatricks meet a number of exotic local characters, including Beatrice Lillie, Ethel Waters, and Eleanor Powell. Although the show contained some amusing sketches and at least one first-class song, "Thief in the Night," sung by Waters, it could not compete with the season's unusually strong musical offerings, which included not only *On Your Toes*, but the Theatre Guild production of Gershwin's *Porgy and Bess*, Billy Rose's circus extravaganza *Jumbo* at the Hippodrome, and the Shuberts' own 1936 reprise of the *Ziegfeld Follies*.

As producers, Lee and J.J. had always been autocrats. By the mid-thirties, however, they were often taking a less central role in their productions. The 1936 *Ziegfeld Follies* was a case in point. Billie Burke received producing credit on the show. The Shuberts were uncredited, although Lee at least was substantially involved. So was a Shubert associate, a ticket broker named Harry Kaufman, whom A.J. Liebling described as "a blocky, Broadway sort of chap with a wide, shining face, who began in the cloak-and-suit business." In addition to his connection with two Broadway ticket agencies, Kaufman became a kind of general manager, talent scout, adviser on box-office matters, and house producer on "Lee's Side." He was involved in the 1936 *Follies* in a hands-on capacity, and would "supervise" (as the phrase went) any number of Shubert shows in the years to come.

Eleanor Powell, who appeared as a solo tap dancer in At Home Abroad *(1935); and Beatrice Lillie and Herb Williams in a scene from the show. (The photograph of Powell shows her at an earlier time, when she was a member of the Albertina Rasch Dancers.)* At Home Abroad *was directed, designed, and costumed by twenty-eight-year-old Vincente Minnelli, who also wrote some of the sketch material. Minnelli, who was born into a tent-show family, had previously worked as a set and costume designer at the Paramount Theatre and as art director of Radio City Music Hall. Earlier in the season he had been one of the designers of Lee and J.J.'s 1934* Ziegfeld Follies*. At Home Abroad *was the first Broadway directing assignment for Minnelli, whom a newspaper interview called "a big gift to the revue."*

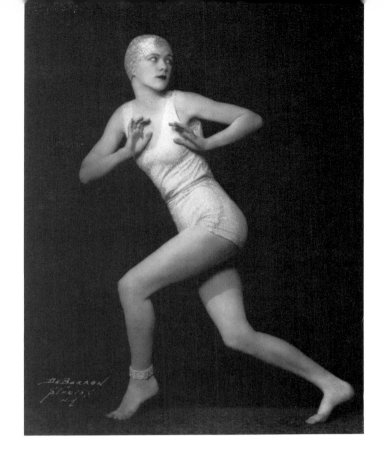

The Ziegfeld Follies of 1936: *Bob Hope and Eve Arden; Gypsy Rose Lee, who appeared in a second edition of the show, replacing Arden; and ballet dancer Harriet Hoctor. Although the 1934 and 1936 Shubert versions of Ziegfeld's famous revues were very different in character from the earlier shows created by Ziegfeld himself, they were among the strongest of Lee and J.J.'s revues. And as musical theatre historian Stanley Green points out, the 1936 version "was generally conceded to be an even better* Follies *than the last one." Green suggests, however, that the much-heralded appearance of Josephine Baker in the 1936 show turned out to be a bit of a dud—it "provoked so even-tempered a critic as Brooks Atkinson to fume, 'Her singing is only a squeak in the dark and her dancing is only the pain of an artist.'"*

The new *Follies,* directed by John Murray Anderson, with choreography by Robert Alton and George Balanchine, was a considerable success, altogether running for some 250 performances at the Winter Garden. In its original edition, which opened in January of 1936, the show brought back, among others, Fanny Brice and Eve Arden from the 1934 cast, composer Vernon Duke and lyricist Ira Gershwin. Important additions included Gertrude Niesen, Harriet Hoctor, Judy Canova, Josephine Baker, the Nicholas Brothers, and Bob Hope. Hope and Arden offered the classic "I Can't Get Started with You," about a big man about town with a problem about romance. "I've got a house, it's a show place," Hope sang, "But I can't get no place with you." The show closed in the spring when Brice fell ill. In the fall, when it reopened, Bobby Clark replaced Hope, with Jane Pickens taking over Gertrude Niesen's role, and Gypsy Rose Lee the Eve Arden part.

Equally successful, with an initial run of 237 performances, was *The Show Is On,* a revue put together at the Winter Garden by Vincente Minnelli, starring Bert Lahr and Beatrice Lillie. Their material was provided by a seemingly endless list of extraordinary sketch writers, lyricists, and song writers, among them Vernon Duke, Moss Hart, George and Ira Gershwin, Howard Dietz, Arthur Schwartz, Hoagy Carmichael, Richard Rodgers, Yip Harburg, and Harold Arlen. In a sense, *The Show Is On* was Minnelli's sequel to *At Home Abroad.* Like its predecessor, the new show had a loosely conceived storyline—this time, show business around the world—but it was incidental to the antics of Lahr and Lillie. Lahr, in the role of movie star "Ronald Traylor," parodied the Mrs. Simpson–Prince of Wales affair, and Lillie impersonated a temperamental star and a music-hall vamp, tossing garters to the audience from a crescent-moon swing.

A classic moment was Lahr's "Song of the Woodman," a send-up of hammy baritones, written by Harburg and Arlen, and itself a kind of sequel to the comic's famous "Things" from *Life Begins at 8:40.* Lahr, dressed in a lumberjack's outfit, with axe in hand, stands next to a pathetic stick of a tree. Periodically, throughout the song, he is inundated with woodchips thrown at him from offstage. In *Notes on a Cowardly Lion,* Lahr's son John quotes Lillie on what she believed to be the essence of one of his father's finest routines. "He took all that

The Show Is On *(1936): Bert Lahr, Beatrice Lillie, and Helene Ecklund, later John Shubert's wife; a Vincente Minnelli design for the show; Lahr in the "Song of the Woodman" sketch; and Beatrice Lillie. The Show Is On was among the last of the great Broadway revues. Two years earlier Minnelli had commented to an interviewer about the problems facing the revue form. Not only were spectators far more sophisticated in their expectations, but "the movies have been so lavish with stars that audiences are beginning to demand definite personalities to lead even the most routine parts of a stage production. . . . And with so many artists on the West Coast working for the motion pictures, it complicates the task of casting a show which must have from three to five stars in order to be a success."*

wood in the face with great dignity. There was no slapstick—and if there was—it was dignified. That's me, that's me—whatever happens I rise above it."

Critics loved *The Show Is On*, which has been called the last of the classic revues. They were less enthusiastic about two throwbacks to the operetta tradition, *Frederika* and *Three Waltzes*. *Frederika*, which mined yet again the "great man" theme, ran for three months at the Imperial, starting in February of 1937. The show, with music by Franz Lehar, was an adaptation of a German original from the late twenties. It starred Dennis King as the young Johann Wolfgang von Goethe and Helen Gleason as his first love Frederika, who comes to realize that the pair are mismatched and that for Goethe's sake she must pretend to be in love with another.

Three Waltzes opened on Christmas day, 1937, at the Majestic, with Kitty Carlisle and Michael Bartlett. The show was another of the "three generation" operettas, with unrequited love in 1865 and 1900, and the possibility of a suitably happy ending in 1937 for the grandchildren of the original lovers. *Three Waltzes* did contain a rather charming musical device: the first two acts used period music by Johann Strauss and Johann Strauss, Jr., and the third act new compositions by Oscar Straus. In fact, *Three Waltzes* had been a considerable success in Europe, but the rather heavy-handed American adaptation managed only a four-month run.

By the late thirties, Lee and J.J.'s well-known frugality had reached epic proportions. Sets and costumes were recycled endlessly, as were their favorite shows and songs. Like so many others, they were strongly affected by the trauma of the Depression, and they tried to wring every last dollar from their remaining investments and properties. Unlike Ziegfeld, who had spent lavishly on his costumes, Lee and J.J. were famous for what designers—and the critics—felt was excessive thrift with the visual elements of their shows. The costumes and sets, often inexpensive to start with, were used and reused until decidedly past their best. Then they were meticulously stored away in Shubert warehouses just in case one more show appeared in which they could be recycled. In later years, in addition to their former movie studio in Fort Lee, which had been converted to use as a

A costume design by William Weaver for Frederika *(1937); and two designs by Connie De Pinna for* Three Waltzes *(1937). J.J. never gave up his enthusiasm for operetta. In a press release for* Frederika, *soberly headed "MR. J.J. SHU-BERT TALKS OF THE THEATRE," he is given credit "for the daring gesture to determine whether the monopoly of jazz and the saxophone in the theatre is at an end and a hearing awaits more conventional and melodious musical entertainment." Not unexpectedly, J.J. finds that his recent summer revivals of operettas have demonstrated that he was right. "'The interest and enthusiasm centering in those performances convinced me that an effort should be made to restore this delightful amusement form to the theatre. Fundamentally, the public has not changed as demonstrated by my son, John, fresh from Harvard, and representative of the young generation.'"*

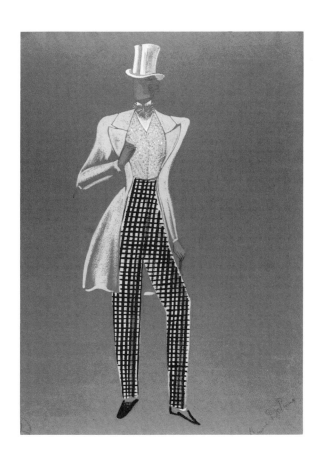

warehouse, the Shuberts owned several other shops and storehouses, and a building in Greenwich Village where scenery was built and painted, props and electrical equipment housed, and costumes for Shubert shows were made.

According to John Shubert, the Village building was totally inadequate, and he was of the opinion that it would have been cheaper for his father and uncle to hire outside firms to handle all of the technical aspects of their shows. But Lee and J.J. were convinced that the warehouse was essential for storing props and scenery used by their road companies. In any case, as he pointed out, they "hated to throw anything away, and the storehouse eventually was packed to the rafters. . . . Father, who adored every square foot of this large building, had carefully memorized every item in it, and refused to let anyone throw so much as a scrap of wood away without his written approval." In fact, Lee and J.J. for years derived considerable income from renting out their old costumes and settings, many of them well beyond the age of dignified retirement.

Lee and J.J.'s favorite shows—mostly the shop-worn operettas from the teens and twenties—were still being trotted out year after year for tours and summer stock. For three years, at the beginning of the decade, J.J. and his nephew Milton had run successful summer seasons at the huge St. Louis Municipal Opera in Forest Park. The stock ventures at the end of the thirties were produced by J.J. and John at Jones Beach and Randall's Island in New York, and in Louisville, Kentucky.

The low-budget Jones Beach shows, which took place for several years at a large open-air theatre in a state park near New York City, were a co-production venture with Fortune Gallo, the impresario of the San Carlo Opera Company. The San Carlo was an established if not precisely revered Manhattan company which had offered operas at popular prices for some years in parks and stadiums. The Shubert–San Carlo collaboration was incorporated under the rather grandiose name of the People's National Academy of Allied Theatrical Arts, and its souvenir programs billed the venture in terms of artistic uplift. "The theatre," the program announced, "must return to its former glory and activity not only because of its tradition as an imperishable medium of expression, but, also to reflect the advancing trends in the progress of civilization and to provide a training and proving ground for the people of the stage."

On Broadway, meanwhile, Lee and J.J. were producing few straight plays. Lee offered Tallulah Bankhead in a relatively uninteresting George Kelly play, *Reflected Glory,* at the Morosco for four

Tallulah Bankhead in Reflected Glory, *1936. The play was not a success. Although Bankhead was praised, as usual, for her vitality and glamour in a play clearly designed—as usual—to show off those qualities, critics found her performance far superior to the vehicle created to display her. "It is my guess," Richard Watts wrote, "that Miss Bankhead is an excellent actress, but it is hard to be certain in the matter. Only in 'Rain' have New York playgoers been given an opportunity to see her in a part which demanded a real characterization."* Reflected Glory, *on the other hand, merely "gives its star an opportunity to present a one-person show that could well make Miss Ruth Draper and Joe Cook jealous, and you can imagine how Miss Bankhead takes advantage of it."*

months, beginning in September 1936, and Lee and J.J. presented a company from Dublin's Abbey Theatre at the Ambassador for 85 performances, starting in October 1937. But the emphasis throughout the rest of the thirties was clearly to be on musicals. Two of them, *Between the Devil* and *You Never Know*, were failures or close to it. Two others, *Hooray for What!* and the legendary *Hellzapoppin'*, were to be among the Shuberts' most satisfying successes.

Between the Devil was a Dietz and Schwartz musical with Jack Buchanan and Vilma Ebsen in the cast, which ran for 93 performances at the Imperial, starting in December 1937. The show, about the adventures of an unwitting bigamist, contained several excellent songs, including "I See Your Face Before Me," "By Myself," and a great comedy number, "Triplets." But *Between the Devil* never seemed to attract audiences or interest the critics very much, most of whom found it crudely farcical and out of date.

Cole Porter's *You Never Know* opened at the Winter Garden in September 1938. It was, by Porter's own admission, his worst show. *You Never Know* had begun as a straight play by the German writer Siegfried Geyer, with the usual aristocrats disguised as their servants, and vice versa. For reasons that now seem obscure, the script had several reincarnations, including an English translation by P.G. Wodehouse, *By Candlelight,* with Gertrude Lawrence and Leslie Howard, and a Viennese musical, *Bei Kerzenlicht*, by Karl Farkas. The Shubert show was loosely based on the musical, but most of the numbers were interpolated by Porter. Some of his contributions were good—notably the classic "At Long Last Love"—and the show featured a strong cast that included Clifton Webb, Libby Holman, and Lupe Velez. But, as with *Between the Devil*, critics found *You Never Know* old-fashioned and largely unimpressive, and it closed after 78 performances.

Hooray for What!, a musical starring famed comic Ed Wynn, was another matter altogether. With a run of more than six months at the Winter Garden, beginning in December 1937, the show was a solid success. In part, its popularity may be attributed to the rapidly worsening world political situation. *Hooray for What!*, a parable about the international arms race, certainly had more than a hint of serious social criticism in its lyrics by Yip Harburg, and book by Howard

Rex O'Malley, Lupe Velez and Clifton Webb in Cole Porter's You Never Know, *1938.* You Never Know *turned out to be a weak musical, with a cliché-ridden comic-opera plot about a romance between two servants impersonating aristocrats. Porter himself despised the show. Lee, J.J., and John brought in George Abbott to doctor it on the road, and interpolated the popular dance team of Grace and Paul Hartman in an attempt to add some vitality to the proceedings. But nothing seemed to help.* You Never Know *did badly on Broadway, but it appears to have been popular for some years with summer stock companies because of Porter's impressive reputation.*

Lindsay and Russel Crouse, although some of its bite disappeared in tryouts, along with an antiwar ballet by Agnes de Mille. The story involves a horticulturist named Chuckles who invents a gas to kill apple worms which is also lethal to human beings. Immediately, all of the European super powers send their agents to steal the formula; the

Ed Wynn in Howard Lindsay and Russel Crouse's Hooray for What!, *1937; and Wynn (at center) and Vivian Vance, who replaced Kay Thompson prior to the opening. Vance who had worked in amateur theatre in her hometown of Albuquerque, New Mexico, did a cabaret act in New York prior to her first major breaks in the theatre: understudying Ethel Merman in* Anything Goes *(1934), which was directed by Lindsay, and in a Lindsay and Crouse vehicle for Merman,* Red, Hot and Blue *(1936). After a long career in theatre and film, Vance would achieve fame in another medium as Ethel Mertz, Lucille Ball's ex-vaudevillian landlady in the "I Love Lucy" television series.*

one who manages to do so, however, copies it backwards and invents a form of laughing gas that promotes brotherly love.

The show's topical message aside, attendance was certainly stimulated by the nationwide popularity of its star. Wynn ("The Perfect Fool"), long a favorite in vaudeville and musical comedy, had received coast-to-coast acclaim beginning in 1932 as the star of the Texaco-sponsored "The Fire Chief" radio show. A few critics, in fact, saw him as the only major asset of *Hooray for What!* ("Hooray principally for Ed Wynn," wrote Brooks Atkinson of the *Times*). But for the most part, both Wynn and the show were well received by critics and audiences. Behind *Hooray for What!* was an unusually talented team that included Harburg as lyricist and Harold Arlen as composer. Lindsay directed, and settings and costumes were by Vincente Minnelli and Raoul Pène du Bois respectively. The show's music was not outstanding overall, but there were several first-rate songs, including "Down with Love" and "Moanin' in the Mornin'," sung by the young Vivian Vance.

The Shubert sensation of the late thirties was a bizarre show called *Hellzapoppin'*. The creators of this phenomenon were a vaudeville comedy team, Ole Olsen and Chic Johnson, who had begun working together in the mid-teens. By the thirties Olsen and Johnson were a popular act, but little more than that. They had made a few minor-league films and had appeared extensively in vaudeville and in several revues, including the *Ziegfeld Follies of 1922*. The direct origin of *Hellzapoppin'* was a "stage show" or "unit show" which the team presented between films at motion picture theatres in the West and Midwest, beginning in the late twenties. Basically, their unit show was vaudeville-style "nut" comedy—slapstick of the lowest common denominator. Olsen and Johnson would later refer to their approach to comedy as "gonk," which they interpreted as "hokum with raisins."

A nightclub owner named Nils T. Granlund introduced Lee Shubert to Olsen and Johnson's hour-long unit show, which was playing in Philadelphia. Lee encouraged the pair to add enough material to bring the show's running time up to two hours, and in September of 1938 the full-length *Hellzapoppin'* opened at the Forty-sixth Street Theatre. Olsen and Johnson were the producers, not the Shuberts,

Hellzapoppin' (1938): Ole Olsen and Chic Johnson in a publicity shot; the Forty-sixth Street Theatre during the run of the show; a souvenir program cover; cast members from the show; and a photograph of Wallace Beery and a chorus girl doing the "Boomps-a-daisy" in the aisle. Olsen and Johnson, the creators of the eccentric and wildly successful revue, pointed out in a New York Times interview that "the critics laughed when they sat down at Hellzapoppin' the opening night, but (with a few notable exceptions) they got up again and said it was a 'bust' . . . . Fate, however, apparently took a look at the ranks of the unemployed and decided to give us a break, and business began to pick up to a point that we grossed $19,000 the first week—the poorest week the show has had since opening in New York."

although in fact it was Shubert money that financed the production, and it was staged by Shubert personnel. *Hellzapoppin'* would turn out to be a remarkable investment; the show, which would later transfer to the Winter Garden, would eventually run for more than three years.

In several important ways *Hellzapoppin'* was an anomaly. For one thing, the madcap comedy, complete with continual pistol shots, hula dancers, fruit tossed into the audience, and men in gorilla suits, was unlike anything that revue audiences of the thirties were used to. Not that the premise was a new one. A. J. Liebling would note in his profile of the Shuberts that *Hellzapoppin'* was "not so much an innovation as a type of fast, unsubtle comedy which had been absent from Broadway so long that by 1938 it was new to a whole generation of playgoers."

Beyond that, the critical response to one of the greatest hit shows of all time was almost uniformly unenthusiastic. Brooks Atkinson wrote in the *New York Times:* "Deciding that it might be a good idea to put on a show, Olsen and Johnson stood on a corner of the street and stopped every third man. Those were their actors. Taking an old broom they went up to the attic and swept out all the gags in sight. Those were the jokes." The only important dissenting voice among the reviewers was the *Daily Mirror* critic Walter Winchell, who, for whatever reason, continually plugged the show in his columns and on his radio program.

But Winchell and word of mouth were enough to turn *Hellzapoppin'* inexplicably into the stuff of Broadway legend. The predictable aftermath was a rash of vaudeville-style revues throughout the remainder of the thirties and the early forties. Several of them were reprises by Olsen and Johnson themselves, and a number of them—both by Olsen and Johnson and their imitators—would be produced by Lee and J.J.

VI
FINALE

I say money, money, money.
I say money, money, money and
I say hot dog! I say yes, no, and
I say money, money, money and I say
turkey sandwich and I say grape juice.
  CARMEN MIRANDA
  Interview in the
  New York *World Telegraph*

Ole Olsen and Chic Johnson would produce or perform in four more shows for the Shuberts, all of them more or less in the same vein as *Hellzapoppin'*. There was a book musical, *Sons o' Fun*, in 1941, *Count Me In* the next year, and *Laffing Room Only* in 1944. A highly successful 1939 Olsen and Johnson revue called *Streets of Paris* would run for eight months, starting in June, at the Broadhurst Theatre. Like *Hellzapoppin'*, the show was staged by Edward Duryea Dowling, who by this time was virtually the Shubert house director. A second Shubert institution, Robert Alton, choreographed the show. The music and lyrics were by the talented team of Jimmy McHugh and Al Dubin, and the great Irene Sharaff designed the costumes.

In no small part, the show's success was the result of a Lee Shubert discovery who would become one of the entertainment sensations of the forties, Carmen Miranda. Not that *Streets of Paris* was without other talented performers. Unlike *Hellzapoppin'*, it was packed with first-rate entertainers, including Bobby Clark, who had replaced Bob Hope in the Shubert's *Ziegfeld Follies of 1936;* another Shubert veteran, Luella Gear; the young Gower Champion; the French star Jean Sablon; and the popular comedy team of Bud Abbott and Lou Cos-

 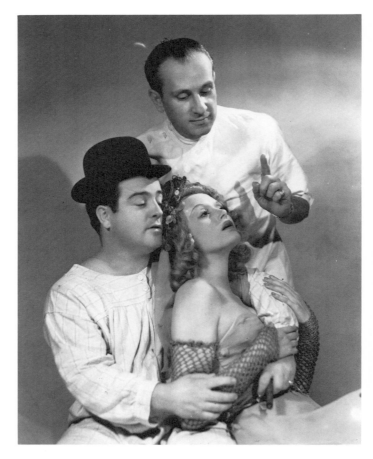

Carmen Miranda in The Streets of Paris *(1939); and Bud Abbott and Lou Costello with Della Lind in the same show. The* Streets of Paris *was produced by Olsen and Johnson, the perpetrators of the zany* Hellzapoppin' *of 1938, which it resembled in its frenetic lack of inhibition. Like Miranda, Abbott and Costello became darlings of the critics—and shortly American comedy institutions. "Abbott," Brooks Atkinson wrote, "is the overbearing master-mind whose feverish, impatient guidance of the conversation produces the crisis. Costello is the short, fat, he-who-gets-slapped. He is a moon-faced zany with wide, credulous eyes, a high voice and puffy hands that struggle in futile gestures. Both men work themselves into a state of feverish excitement that is wonderful to behold."*

tello, in their only appearance on Broadway. But more than any other performer, it was Carmen Miranda who put over *Streets of Paris*.

While on a holiday cruise, Lee had found Miranda singing in a nightclub in Rio. In May of 1939 his discovery arrived in New York, attended by every conceivable kind of press hoopla, and began to set the entertainment industry on its ear ("Brazilian Heat Wave Radiates," cried a headline in the *New York Sun*). Miranda's effect on American popular culture was immediate and dramatic; fashion designers appropriated the star's six-inch heels, fruit-bowl turbans, and ropes of multicolored beads, and Miranda-imitators were soon a standard act in nightclubs across the country.

In *Streets of Paris*, Miranda performed at the end of the first act, finishing her number—which was filled with eccentric movement and bizarre gesture—by bringing out an identically dressed midget to sing and dance with her. The number became an overnight sensation. "Hi yi," she sang, "hi yi, / Have you ever danced in the tropics, / In that hazy lazy-like, / Kind of crazy-like, / South American way?" The *Journal-American* critic John Anderson called it "the greatest event in our relations with South America since the Panama Canal."

The "samba-singing sensation" was to appear again in the Shuberts' December 1941 Olsen and Johnson show at the Winter Garden, *Sons o' Fun*, along with the young singer Ella Logan. In the meantime, Miranda had been in Hollywood, which provided her with outrageous new jokes. In a routine with the two comics, Miran-

Ole Olsen and Chic Johnson with an unidentified performer in Sons o' Fun, *1941. A souvenir program pointed out that "Olsen and Johnson bashfully admit that their latest opus makes their fabulous* Hellzapoppin' *seem somewhat like a quiet evening at home." Audiences adored the new show, which had a long Broadway run and toured extensively. A Cleveland critic agreed that* Sons o' Fun *"outpops* Hellzapoppin' *. . . though we never thought anything possibly could be whackier than their first edition of what they call unorthodox monkey business. This show actually has more horseplay, and, of course, more laughs. And its costuming and sets are better."*

da pointed out that she had met a number of movie celebrities, including "Clark Gabble, Mickey Mice, Spencer Trachis, and Macaroni." "With cheese?" Johnson asked. "No, MGM." "Oh, you mean Mickey Rooney." In spite of—or perhaps because of—such material, the show, which marked Miranda's final Broadway appearance, would run for an astonishing two years.

While Miranda belted out "The South American Way" in *The Streets of Paris,* near by the young Imogene Coca was regaling audiences with a parody of it, written by Sylvia Fine. Called "The Soused American Way," the number featured Coca as a cut-rate Brazilian Bombshell, with a turban topped with vegetables and ears of corn dangling from her waist. Her song was designed to entice several rustics back to the country. "Hi Lem," she intoned, "Hi Zeke, / Have you ever been to a barn dance? / Where city slickers / Let down their knickers / That Soused American Way."

The show in which this rural effusion appeared was *The Straw Hat Revue,* which ran for nine weeks at the Ambassador, starting in September of 1939. *The Straw Hat Revue* began as a summer entertainment conceived by Max Liebman (later to become famous as the producer of television's "Your Show of Shows"), with music and lyrics by Fine and James Shelton. It had been conceived at the theatre at Camp Tamiment in the Poconos, where Liebman had established an outstanding summer stock operation. Harry Kaufman spotted Liebman's show there and convinced Lee to transport it to Broadway—in no small part because it could be cheaply and easily mounted. Kaufman and Lee, however, were not convinced that all of the Tamiment material was suitable for a Broadway audience. They cut out several numbers (notably "The Yiddish *Mikado,*" a fabled sendup of the recent fad for ethnic versions of the Gilbert and Sullivan operetta), and inserted new songs and sketches, which added little to the show.

But much good material remained, including a song that was to become a classic and to mark the beginning of a great show business career. The song was "Anatole of Paris," sung by the man whom Fine was shortly to marry, Danny Kaye, impersonating a deranged French couturier ("I'm Anatole of Paris / I shriek with chic.") Another number in the show was a funny—and quite telling—satire called "The Great Chandelier." The sketch was named for the crystal chandelier that seemed always to appear on stage at some point during the

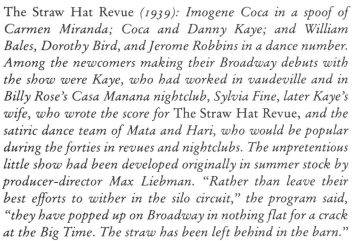

The Straw Hat Revue (1939): Imogene Coca in a spoof of Carmen Miranda; Coca and Danny Kaye; and William Bales, Dorothy Bird, and Jerome Robbins in a dance number. Among the newcomers making their Broadway debuts with the show were Kaye, who had worked in vaudeville and in Billy Rose's Casa Manana nightclub, Sylvia Fine, later Kaye's wife, who wrote the score for The Straw Hat Revue, and the satiric dance team of Mata and Hari, who would be popular during the forties in revues and nightclubs. The unpretentious little show had been developed originally in summer stock by producer-director Max Liebman. "Rather than leave their best efforts to wither in the silo circuit," the program said, "they have popped up on Broadway in nothing flat for a crack at the Big Time. The straw has been left behind in the barn."

Shubert operettas that still endlessly criss-crossed America each year during the theatre season. The sketch, set in Venice, featured a masked gondolier, spies, mistaken identities, a quartet of maidens named Mitzi, Titzi, Kitzi, and Fritzi, and of course the ubiquitous Great Chandelier. Wolcott Gibbs suggested in the *New Yorker* that the number "ought to (but won't) protect us from any future renditions of feeble-minded Viennese operettas."

In fact, Gibbs was fairly safe on one count; by now even the Shuberts had virtually given up producing new operettas, although they still continued to retread the old ones for the road. An uninteresting exception was *Night of Love,* which managed a week's run early in 1941. By the forties, Lee and J.J. were in fact producing relatively little. One of their offerings, *Keep Off the Grass,* a mediocre revue with a splendid cast, played for six weeks in the spring of 1940. The show featured the likes of Jimmy Durante, Ray Bolger, José Limon, Larry Adler, the famous circus clown Emmet Kelley, Jane Froman, and Ilka Chase. The score was by the seasoned professional Jimmy McHugh, and George Balanchine choreographed. All in all, the results ought to have been better than they were. *Walk with Music,* a book musical which ran for 55 performances at the Barrymore during the 1939–1940 season, had lyrics by Johnny Mercer and music by Hoagy Carmichael, as well as several talented performers, including Kitty Carlisle and Frances Williams. But the book, about three farm girls who seek their fortunes in Palm Beach, was weak, and constant interpolations and changes weakened it even further.

Like his father and his uncle, John Shubert continued to produce in a small way in the early forties. In January of 1942, for example, he presented *Johnny on a Spot,* by playwright Charles MacArthur, a much-rewritten comedy that centered on smuggling a governor's corpse out of a bordello. The undistinguished show, which featured two well-known actors, Keenan Wynn and Will Geer, played the Plymouth for a total run of four days. Shortly John would leave Broadway—probably with a sigh of relief—to become a captain in the army. As chairman and Chief Editor of the Material and Writers Committee of the United Services Organization (U.S.O.), his job was to assemble a series of "Soldier Shows" source books for members of the armed forces who were producing revues at military installations.

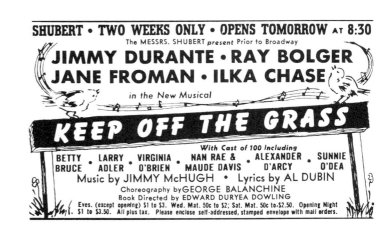

Advertisement for an out-of-town tryout for Keep Off the Grass, 1940; and a dance number from the revue, choreographed by George Balanchine, who had also provided dances for the first Shubert edition of the Ziegfeld Follies. The show did not generate much enthusiasm from the critics, although the New Yorker offered it a kind of backhanded tribute when it lauded "Mr. Durante, Mr. Bolger, Miss Ilka Chase, and their associates, who, dealing with such fine old chestnuts as tree surgery, Cafe Society, and the Roosevelt family, accomplished the feat of supplying in person a humor that certainly didn't exist in the script."

Will Geer and Keenan Wynn in Johnny on a Spot *(1942); and a page from a program for the ill-fated production. The farce was John Shubert's maiden effort as a producer, and it was badly received. The Shubert press chief, Claude Greneker, sent a packet of reviews to J.J. on the day after the opening, noting, with a certain delicacy, in a cover letter that "the morning reviews of 'Johnny on a Spot,' the farce adapted by Charles MacArthur and directed by him, and produced by John Shubert, are anything but good. Much of the failure of the play to be as funny as it might have been, was laid to Mr. MacArthur's direction."*

THE PLYMOUTH THEATRE
PLYMOUTH THEATRE CORPORATION

FIRE NOTICE: The exit indicated by a red light and sign, nearest to the seat you occupy is the shortest route to the street.
In the event of fire or other emergency please do not run—WALK TO THAT EXIT.
PATRICK WALSH (No. 1), Fire Commissioner and Chief of Department
It is urged for the comfort and safety of all, that theatre patrons refrain from lighting matches in this theatre.

THE · PLAYBILL · PUBLISHED · BY · THE · NEW · YORK · THEATRE · PROGRAM · CORPORATION

Beginning Thursday, January 8, 1942   ●   Matinees Wednesday and Saturday

JOHN SHUBERT

presents

A New Comedy

JOHNNY ON A SPOT

by

CHARLES MacARTHUR

featuring

KEENAN WYNN   EDITH ATWATER

WILL GEER   DENNIE MOORE   JOSEPH SWEENEY

PAUL HUBER   FLORENCE SUNDSTROM   TITO VUOLO

Staged by Mr. MacArthur

From a story by Parke Levy and Alan Lipscott

Setting and Costumes designed by Frederick Fox

CAST
(In order of appearance)

ST. JOHN .... ROBERT WILLIAMS
McCLURE .... ARTHUR MARLOWE
CHRONICLE REPORTER .... RICHARD KARLAN

The resulting books were basically anthologies of simple sketches, skits, songs, minstrel routines, and the like, drawn from legitimate theatre, vaudeville, and radio, and presented with detailed notes aimed at amateur producers. John was in charge of obtaining material for the series, as well as final editing, and a number of the sketches came from such popular Shubert revues as *Life Begins at 8:40, The Show Is On, Streets of Paris, The Straw Hat Revue*, and the various Shubert editions of the *Ziegfeld Follies*. Meanwhile, at home, Lee was active on various bond drives and benefits, and served as chairman of the Legitimate Theater Campaign for the Army and Navy Emergency Relief, which took collections at theatres in 1942. Many of Lee and J.J.'s wartime activities probably went unnoticed because of their passion for anonymity. Producer John Golden, for example, told columnist Sidney Fields in 1942 that, although most people were not aware of it, the Shuberts had donated the space for the famous Broadway servicemen's club, the Stage Door Canteen, even though they had been offered a large amount of money by a man who wanted to open a nightclub in the space.

In part because of the war, and in part because of flagging energy, Lee and J.J. were producing even less than before. There were New York revivals of Gilbert and Sullivan operettas in 1942 and *The Student Prince* and *Blossom Time* in 1943. But relatively few new shows appeared. Among those that did were several revues presented with an obscure nightclub owner and producer named Clifford Fischer. Basically, the Shubert-Fischer shows were little more than retreaded vaudeville, but they offered theatre-goers a kind of nostalgic, escapist entertainment that seemed to work for a time during the hectic war years.

Priorities of 1942, the first of the shows, opened at the Forty-sixth Street Theatre in March 1942, with Willie Howard, Lou Holtz, and Phil Baker, mostly doing their old material in front of drops from the Shubert warehouses. At discount prices, the show ran for more than 350 performances. The results were so pleasing, in fact, that in April a similar Shubert-Fischer assemblage—this one with William Gaxton, Victor Moore, Hildegarde, Jack Cole and his dance company, and a young performer named Zero Mostel—opened near by at the Forty-fourth Street Theatre under the title *Keep 'Em Laughing*. It was not

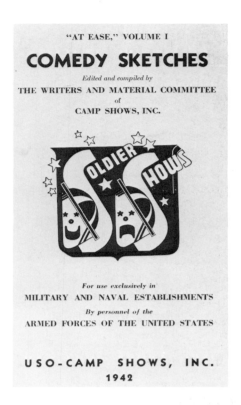

The war years: one of the anthologies of soldier-show sketch material pre-pared under John's direction; John Shubert in uniform; Lee Shubert with military personnel at Broadway's Stage Door Canteen about 1944; and Shu-bert showgirls publicizing a used clothing drive in Chicago. A radio spot for a Shubert show of the period suggests a startling twist on the usual war effort. "Many methods of selling war stamps and bonds have been devised since we got into the big struggle," the copy reads, "but I doubt if one as unique as the one in this new show 'Priorities of 1943' can be found anywhere but in said show. It is the strip tease method and tonight, by the time the young lady attired in stamps had gone as far as the law allows, about fifty dollars worth of stamps had been sold and one $50,000 bond."

particularly successful and was transformed in May into *The Top-Notchers*, without most of its original stars, but with the addition of Gracie Fields to the company. *The Top-Notchers*, in turn, excited no particular interest. Nor did *New Priorities of 1943*, which repeated the nostalgia premise with Harry Richman, Bert Wheeler, and the young comedian Henny Youngman. The show closed after seven weeks, and the brief vaudeville revival of the war years was all but over. There was one last hurrah, however—Lee's ill-fated *Wine, Women and Song.*

Lee and his co-producers, Max Liebman of *Straw Hat Revue* fame and I. W. Herk, the burlesque entrepreneur, tried to cover all possible nostalgic bases by billing *Wine, Women and Song* as a "revue-vaudeville-burlesque show." In fact, the show, which opened at the Ambassador in September of 1942, was unabashedly burlesque. It came about in part as a result of the success of *Priorities of '42*—but more specifically because of producer Mike Todd's *Star and Garter,* which had appeared in June. *Star and Garter* was Todd's successful attempt to capitalize on the recent closing of New York City burlesque houses by Mayor LaGuardia. It featured the classic strippers Gypsy Rose Lee and Georgia Sothern and oldtime comic Bobby Clark; and it would run for a very healthy eighteen months. *Wine, Women and Song* was Lee's characteristic attempt to capitalize on a competitor's already proven idea—an approach that went back as least as far as the Shuberts' imitations of Florenz Ziegfeld's *Follies.* Lee's show, which ran for less than two months, starred several lesser figures—Margie Hart, Jimmy Savo, and Pinkie Lee—and got him into considerable trouble with the police, who closed *Wine, Women and Song* for obscenity and padlocked the Ambassador for almost a year. Herk actually received a short jail sentence for his part in the affair.

The resulting publicity was predictably unpleasant. Perhaps in part as a response to the *Wine, Women and Song* disaster, Lee and J.J. would produce only two more revues during the rest of the war years. There was a brief, largely uninteresting *Ziegfeld Follies of 1943,* with Milton Berle, Arthur Treacher, and Jack Cole, staged by John Murray Anderson and "supervised" by Harry Kaufman. In 1944 came the final Olsen and Johnson epic, *Laffing Room Only,* also directed by Anderson and starring the dance team of Mata and Hari, who had appeared in several other Shubert shows, the old vaudevillians Willie West and McGinty, and Betty Garrett. The show ran for more than 200 performances at the Winter Garden.

There was one book musical, too. With Olsen and Johnson, Lee and J.J. produced a short-lived musical comedy, *Count Me In,* by Walter Kerr, Leo Brady, and Nancy Hamilton. The show, which

William Gaxton, Hildegarde, and Victor Moore in Keep 'Em Laughing *(1942); and an advertisement for* New Priorities of 1943. *The two unexciting shows were produced by the Shuberts and Clifford Fischer. For the most part, neither revue made much of a hit with critics or audiences. But there was one exception. Both shows contained the same extraordinary act, The Bricklayers, which featured fourteen dogs. As* Time *explained it, The Bricklayers "who dump loads of bricks, clamber up and down ladders, act tight, sham dead, ride around on scooters and perform on the trapeze deserve the rare compliment that they might have been invented by Walt Disney." The* Post *called them "the canine wonders of the current theatrical world."*

appeared at the Barrymore in October of 1942 and ran for seven weeks, had a first-rate cast and production staff, including Charles Butterworth, Luella Gear, Mary Healey, Jean Arthur, and Gower Champion and Jeanne Tyler. Howard Bay designed the sets and Irene Sharaff the costumes. But the story was almost swallowed up by incidental variety acts, and the critical response was highly unenthusiastic.

An advertisement for Olsen and Johnson's Laffing Room Only; *and a photograph of Betty Garrett in a scene from the show. Olsen and Johnson's last revue for the Shuberts turned out to be yet another replay of the pair's distinctive and highly successful brand of insanity. As Ted Shane, a feature writer, suggested during the run of the show, for some thirty years Olsen and Johnson had been "making a good living out of the principle that if you rush onstage screaming and fire a machine gun point-blank in the audience's face, that audience—instead of retreating to the nearest Shakespearean revival—will come back for more." "'We're not comedians,' Johnson told an interviewer named Lawrence Perry, 'we are merchandisers of merriment.'"*

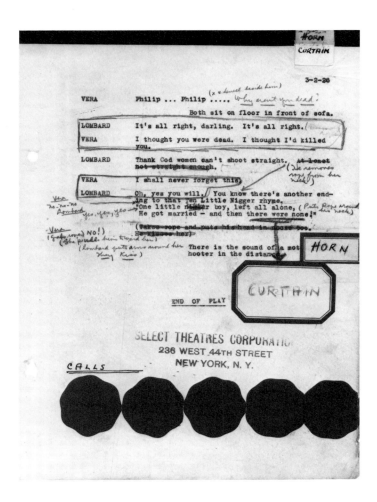

A scene from the Shubert production of Agatha Christie's Ten Little Indians *(1944); and the final page of the prompt script. After a New York run of almost a year, the show toured extensively around the country. In a period when Christie's novels and plays were not particularly well known in America, Lee and J.J.'s press agent, Claude Greneker, was quick to stretch a point with potential audience members to make clear that the play was not just another English mystery. "While serious in intent," his tour release read, 'Ten Little Indians' has a surprising amount of comedy relief. Over in England, the play has been compared to 'Arsenic and Old Lace.'"*

Among the shows presented by Lee and J.J. during their last years as producers were four distinctive straight plays two of which were to become standard college and amateur theatre attractions. Agatha Christie's *Ten Little Indians*, co-produced with Albert de Courville, opened at the Broadhurst in June of 1944 and became an amateur theatre perennial. The play, which had already had a substantial London run, was one of those isolated-country-house mysteries which Christie did so well. It was a great popular success on Broadway, where it managed to run more than 400 performances. *Dark of the*

A scene from the popular "folk" play Dark of the Moon, *which Lee and J.J. produced in 1945 at the Forty-sixth Street Theatre. The play's authors, Howard Richardson and William Berney, who were first cousins, developed the script originally at the University of Iowa, where both men were doing graduate work. The result was a tremendously successful play;* Dark of the Moon *won a Maxwell Anderson award for the best verse drama of 1942, had a good run on Broadway and later on tour, and is still frequently performed. Berney died young, and although Richardson continued to write on his own for some years, he was never able to achieve the same success with another play.*

Moon, a rather self-conscious but powerful "folk" play on the Barbara Allen theme by Howard Richardson and William Berney, played more than 100 performances at the Forty-sixth Street starting in March of 1945. In later years it was—and still is—presented endlessly by high-school and college drama groups.

With de Courville, Lee and J.J. also produced *The Wind Is Ninety* by Ralph Nelson, a strong play, now virtually forgotten, about the ghost of an Air Force officer who returns to visit his family. *The Wind Is Ninety,* which played for fourteen weeks at the Booth, beginning in June of 1945, featured Blanche Yurka, Joyce Van Patten, and the

Wendell Corey, Kirk Douglas, Bert Lytell, Blanche Yurka, Frances Reid in The Wind Is Ninety, *presented at the Booth in 1945. The children are Donald Devlin and Joyce Van Patten.* The Wind Is Ninety *was a fantasy about a World War II flyer killed in the Pacific whose ghost comes home to establish final contact with his family. The show's author, Ralph Nelson, was himself an Air Force officer who had previously won several playwriting competitions. Like* Dark of the Moon, The Wind Is Ninety *was produced by Lee and J.J. in association with Albert de Courville, who also directed. During John Shubert's time in the army, his father and his uncle had produced fewer and fewer shows on their own. Within a few years they would cease to produce altogether.*

young Kirk Douglas. Guthrie McClintic, the husband of actress Katharine Cornell, was co-producer of *You Touched Me* by Tennessee Williams and Donald Windham, based on a story by D.H. Lawrence and starring Edmund Gwenn and Montgomery Clift. Williams called it a "romantic comedy . . . about troubled people but in a funny way." The critical response to *You Touched Me* was mixed, but the play managed a three-month run at the Booth in September of 1945.

There were more than half a dozen unimportant shows after *You Touched Me,* but the end of the Shuberts as producers was very near. Perhaps the end really came with *My Romance* in October of 1948. The show, which ran for fewer than 100 performances at Lee and J.J.'s flagship Shubert Theatre, was a dinosaur of an operetta, based on a play by the long-dead Edward Sheldon, whose work had been important on Broadway almost a half a century earlier. The music, of course, was by Sigmund Romberg. Brooks Atkinson of the *Times* dismissed it out of hand as "pretentious fiddle-faddle" and added a small but pungent essay about the sort of show that had formed the center of the Shuberts' producing careers for so long. *My Romance,* he wrote, "is standard operetta with standard routines and situations that have not changed through the years. At one time the authors and composers may have believed in these ritualized gestures toward stock romance. But they are pure formula now with high society, passionate love that tears the vocal cords apart and sets the basses and drums to roaring in the orchestra pit, a theme song, nobility, elegance and boredom."

If their careers as producers were indeed virtually over, Lee and J.J. were still refusing to be counted out as critical factors in the life of Broadway. They became increasingly active—and increasingly controversial—as ticket brokers, bookers, investors in shows, and theatrical real estate operators. Shortly there would be ticket scandals and government inquiries. In 1946 the Justice Department's Anti-Trust Division began to investigate the Shuberts' United Booking Office, the former vaudeville booking operation, which they now used to book legitimate attractions on the road. The question at hand was whether the Shuberts' interlocking interests constituted a monopoly. Nothing was settled, but the matter was to come up again soon, as were questions about "ice"—illegal ticket sales—in Lee and J.J.'s theatres.

A costume design by Lou Eiselé for Ann Jeffreys in the Shuberts' last operetta, My Romance (1948), based on an Edward Sheldon play from the teens; and a photograph of Jeffreys wearing the Eiselé costume. A program from the pre-Broadway tour optimistically suggested that "'My Romance' is so new that its songs aren't yet familiar to your ears, but professional observers express optimism over the Hit Parade chances of 'Written in Your Hand,' 'Romance,' 'You're Near and Yet So Far,' and 'Magic Moment.'" Whoever the "professional observers" were, they could not have been more wrong; My Romance was fussy and old-fashioned and could only be kept afloat by the Shuberts for fewer than a hundred performances. Shubert operetta was dead and buried.

The leases on the land under the Plymouth, the Broadhurst, the Booth, the Shubert, and Shubert Alley were due to expire in 1952. In November 1948 the Shuberts bought the entire parcel of land for a sum estimated to be between $3,500,000 and $4,000,000. It was reported to be among the largest real estate transactions ever to have taken place in America. The reasons for the purchase are—characteristically—not altogether clear. Certainly Lee and J.J. were aware that they could do without the houses at this point in their careers; their productions had dwindled to a trickle in the last few years. Clearly, they could have used their money in other ways since they had recently created the Sam S. Shubert Foundation to promote the growth of the American theatre. There were rumors, however, that the Astor estate, which owned the land, was planning to sell it to a group that would tear down the theatres—and other theatres near by—and build a motion picture and television complex. Perhaps the theatres on Forty-fourth and Forty-fifth streets were simply too precious to lose: in the aggregate they were Lee and J.J.'s monument; the Shubert Theatre was their monument to Sam; and Shubert Alley was the symbolic center of the Broadway with which they had grown up and which, over the years, they virtually came to control. Or perhaps it was merely a shrewd business decision—or a bit of both.

Richard Wolpe, a Washington, D.C., journalist, saw the complexity of their motives and drew an interesting conclusion. "It matters little," he wrote in November in the *Times-Herald,* "whether the Shuberts were moved by motives of estheticism or commerce. What does matter is that the threat that the Broadway theatrical district would be sold out to the radio-television-movie interests has been met and repulsed." It is ironic, Wolpe continued, "that the two businessmen who have been accused of changing money in the temple of art have come to the rescue of their accusers by saving the very temple they were accused of defiling."

Wolpe went on to talk about public perceptions of Lee and J.J. His conclusions were unflattering but not unilluminating. In fact, they represented the views that had been current for years: the Shubert brothers were "stingy and penny-pinching to chorus people"; they had never produced "anything but the tried, the true, the trite" and "the sure buck maker"; and while "the brothers wouldn't dare to bring their sleazy productions of oldtime operettas into New York,

Lee Shubert (left) and J.J. (right) with an unidentified man. The picture, taken in 1948, is one of two known photographs of the Shubert brothers together; the other was taken during the teens. It was only their passionate devotion to the company they had created and to the memory of their brother Sam that bound the two together toward the end. And perhaps their shared reputation. An old friend, Donald Flamm, said that despite all that Lee and J.J. did for the theatre over the years, "they were constantly criticized, ridiculed and satirized by columnists and drama desk writers. They never received the same respect and acclaim that was accorded to rival producers. Accolades, so it seemed, were reserved for David Belasco, Charles Dillingham, Arthur Hopkins, Daniel Frohman, Flo Ziegfeld . . . and Jed Harris."

they brazenly pan them off on the road." But none of this was news in 1948. Indeed, by now the Shuberts' shrewdness and their eccentric behavior had entered the realm of Broadway mythology.

However much Lee and J.J. might object to such views of themselves, they firmly maintained their right to conduct their lives and their business affairs precisely as they pleased—no matter how mysterious their behavior might seem—without explanation. In 1948, for example, Lee divorced and remarried Marcella Swanson, although it was never absolutely established that he had married her in the first place. In any case, neither he nor she had ever publically mentioned the marriage, which ostensibly took place in Berlin in 1936. Seemingly, all records of their union had been destroyed during the war. It was generally believed that Marcella received a settlement of several million dollars on agreeing to make no further claims on Lee's estate.

On Christmas day, 1953, Lee died at Mount Sinai Hospital of complications arising from a stroke. The funeral, held three days later at Temple Emanu-El on Fifth Avenue, was reportedly attended by

Lee Shubert, Marcella Swanson Shubert, and producer John Golden, a year before Lee's death. By anyone's standards, Lee Shubert was a difficult man to know and understand. Many theatre people of his day were frightened by him, and yet a few hardy souls like his friend Ruth Gordon somehow managed to be amused by his awesome reserve: "You have no idea what it was like to go to the theatre with Mr. Lee Shubert. I mean, I've never been out with royalty, but it must be like that. Everything would stop, the whole theatre held its breath when he walked in. The crowd would whisper and the ushers would fumble around nervously, 'Yes, Mr. Shubert, how are you tonight, Mr. Shubert?' It was like the parting of the waters."

almost 1500 people. The eulogy, by Rabbi Nathan Perilman, addressed the controversy that surrounded Lee. Men like him, Perilman said, invite "the blind idolatry of those who worship at the shrine of success, the persistent inquiry of the curious, the resentment of the disappointed and the cruel barbs of those who delight in destroying legends, old or new." J.J. was not among the mourners; he was said to be too distraught to participate, although he appeared later at Lee's interment in the family mausoleum at Salem Fields Cemetery.

The newspaper stories that appeared at the time of Lee's death all noted his complexity and his tremendous reserve. Most gave Lee his due for his anonymous charities, his support of Broadway during the Depression, and his immense talent as an entrepreneur. A few writers, like Ed Sullivan, expressed genuine affection for him. Sullivan wrote rather plaintively in the *Daily News* that what Lee had always wanted "was the affection of the people of the theatre. From those who knew him well, those who could penetrate the deep shell of his shyness, he received that affection." Others who knew him "only as the colossus of the Shubert empire of theatres," Sullivan said, "were baffled by his reserve. They retaliated with cruel little jokes about the Shuberts. He gave no outward hint of what those mean gags did to him but they actually made him writhe . . . he loved the theatre and the people of the theatre deeply."

In rehearsal at the time Lee died was a play called *The Starcross Story*, with Christopher Plummer, Eva Le Gallienne, and Mary Astor. The play opened at the Royale on January 13, 1954, and closed after one performance. J.J. was never involved with another play, but he would not be idle. Far from it. All of his life-long resentments and insecurities seemed to come to a boil after Lee's death. In the final version of Lee's will, written in 1952, he had dropped J.J. as executor and trustee of his estate, which J.J. bitterly resented. Beyond that, Lee had seen a nephew, Milton, as his heir-apparent; J.J., who disliked Milton intensely, dismissed him from the company. J.J. now became increasingly obsessed with control, requiring elaborate and unnecessary reports from his department heads, and insisting that he personally approve every bill and sign every check, no matter how trifling. He would turn down absolutely routine requests, and employees found it almost impossible to get their work done. "It got so

J.J. Shubert and Muriel Knowles Shubert aboard the Queen Mary, *1953. Donald Flamm said in an interview that he had often thought that "one of J.J.'s problems was that he always lived in the shadow of his brother Lee." And yet he seemed to feel a certain odd concern for Lee. Once, in the early days of commercial airline flights, Lillian Greneker, the wife of the Shuberts' press chief, went to Newark Airport to pick up Lee and her husband, who were coming in on a flight from California. "I saw J.J. arrive in a great big car.... As soon as the plane touched the ground and Mr. Lee stepped off, J.J.... drove off. J.J. just wanted to make absolutely sure that his brother was alive."*

bad," an old stagehand recalled, "that people would offer to swap you a lightbulb for two rolls of toilet paper."

In 1955 the Supreme Court ruled that the Shuberts were subject to anti-trust laws—which the lower courts had previously said was not the case. In February of the following year, J.J. was forced to sign a consent decree which required him, in effect, to stop booking and to sell off a dozen Shubert theatres in six cities around the country. He did so with the greatest reluctance, of course, reminding the theatre world in a press release that although he would honor the decree, he had his doubts "as to whether some of its provisions will not hurt rather than benefit the legitimate theatre." That was as far as he went; by now, J.J.'s health was declining and John was reluctantly taking over more and more of the company's daily operation, assisted by his second cousin, Lawrence Shubert Lawrence, Jr. In January 1961, John produced another show, *Julia, Jake and Uncle Joe*, starring Claudette Colbert, which closed after a single performance. It was to be the end of Shubert producing for many years to come; for all intents and purposes John was now simply in the theatre real estate business.

Not two years later, in November of 1962, John died of a heart attack on a train bound for Florida. J.J., whose health had failed during the past few years, never knew that John had died. In many ways, his son had become his own antithesis—a gentle, unassuming, rather troubled man, who, all in all, would rather have been a carpenter than the head of a multi-million-dollar corporation. But it was to become clear that there were touches of J.J.'s stubbornness and eccentricity about John.

Services had been set for Frank Campbell's, a funeral home on the Upper East Side, when a letter was found which suggested that John had had very different plans. According to his wishes, the funeral was switched to the Majestic Theatre. At the Majestic the set for *Camelot* was draped with black velour curtains and John's coffin, covered with a blanket of roses, was placed center stage. Next to it was a leather chair in which John's wife Eckie sat mute, dressed in black, as producer Roger Stevens delivered a eulogy and several Shubert executives read passages from the Bible. There were more than 1200 people in

«ДЖУЛИЯ, ДЖЕЙН И ДЯДЯ ДЖО»

A program (with the play title in Russian) for John Shubert's ill-starred production of Julia, Jake and Uncle Joe *(1961), starring Claudette Colbert. The play was based on a book by Oriana Atkinson, the wife of the then-retired* New York Times *critic. The pair had spent ten months in Moscow during the mid-forties, where Brooks Atkinson served as a foreign correspondent for his newspaper. The book was widely praised as a unique account of Russia during the Stalin era. The play based on it, however, was distinctly not a success. Archie Thompson, who assisted John on the show, recalled that his boss had "produced it on the assurance from a major movie studio that they would buy it. But when they saw it they didn't."*

attendance at the funeral—an event which, even by Broadway's liberal standards, was somewhat out of the ordinary. But that was not the end of it. It soon turned out that John had apparently obtained a Mexican divorce from Eckie and that, at the time of his death, he had been on his way to visit his new "wife," by whom he had had two children. The result was a protracted lawsuit, as a result of which Eckie was declared to be John's legal wife and heir.

Meanwhile, on December 26, 1963, J.J. died. His mind was virtually gone and he was unaware of all that had taken place in the last several years. His funeral, like Lee's, was at Temple Emanu-El, and the eulogy, once again, was delivered by Rabbi Nathan Perilman.

John Shubert and his wife Eckie, probably during the 1950s. J.J. kept up a voluminous and apparently more or less one-sided correspondence with John toward the end of John's life and his own. Clearly, J.J. was anxious to pass the reins to his son, but he was never totally able to do so until his health failed completely. "You must remember I have carried on this business right from its inception," he wrote to John in January of 1959. "Then when my brother, and your Uncle, the late Sam Shubert, was taken from us, I had to do all the work with the exception of the work your late Uncle Lee did. He was good on various matters and took care of them but I attended to the operation of this business and the bringing of this business to the condition that it is in today, which will be in your hands at some future time."

J.J. Shubert's funeral. In one of his last letters to John, J.J. recalls with incredible vividness a moment more than half a century earlier that haunted him for the rest of his life—Sam's death. "It made a wreck of our family," he wrote. "Sam was our mother's favorite. She never got over it and she always carried Sam's picture around her neck. I called Erlanger a murderer, said that he was responsible for the death of my brother. I told Erlanger I would get even with him and I lived to see the day that we put him off his throne. It took time but I never gave up, and every time I came in sight of him I told him off. . . . Your late Uncle Lee said it was hurting us, and maybe it did, but I had the satisfaction of calling the bastard what he was. He would never come face to face with me and your Uncle Lee made me finally desist, but I never forgave him."

J.J.'s death, Perilman suggested, brought with it a blessing and a release. For too long he had "walked deep in the valley of the shadow." Perilman deftly touched on the well-known contradictions in J.J.'s personality. He pointed to his "painful" shyness, his anonymous philanthropies, his devotion to Sam's memory, and to the fact that "when he was disappointed or felt betrayed by another, he withdrew his attention and friendship and could be adamantine in a relationship which once had been warm and deeply affectionate." As he had in Lee's eulogy, Perilman spoke of the penalties of becoming "a legend in one's own lifetime" and of being obliged "to live to see that legend embellished by the imaginative, exaggerated by the sycophant, challenged and pried into by the curious, and denigrated by those whose only need is to destroy them."

Yet, undisputably, Perilman said, the Shubert brothers' contribution had been a unique and remarkable one. "Broadway is more than the name of a meandering avenue running from the Battery to Yonkers," he said, and "Broadway's very locale was determined by the choice which these fabulous brothers made over a half a century ago. Where they led, all the rest were bound to follow."

The years that followed J.J.'s death were difficult ones. Lawrence Shubert Lawrence, Jr., a great-nephew of Lee and J.J., was the titular head of the company for almost a decade. In 1972, the Shubert board replaced him with a trio of executive directors, Gerald Schoenfeld and Bernard Jacobs, who had been the company's attorneys for many years, and Irving Goldman, a longtime associate of J.J.'s. (Goldman later would be indicted for perjury and bribery and be dismissed by the company foundation.) For the first time in its history, the Shubert Organization was not run by a member of the Shubert family. At the time, there was considerable controversy about the supposed "takeover" of the company by its attorneys, who, some old Broadway hands felt, knew nothing about the theatre. But in 1977, in an interview with Tom McMorrow in *New York Theatre Review*, Schoenfeld firmly pointed out that if "you represented J.J. you had to be there morning, noon, and night. And to defend them in an anti-trust suit, which we did, you had to know every minute detail of the business. I'd like to match my knowledge with one of those people who say we're not theatre men."

The theatre that Schoenfeld and Jacobs inherited was in serious trouble. By the early seventies, the Times Square district was in decline, the road was virtually moribund, and there were rumors that

Bernard Jacobs and Gerald Schoenfeld, the current President and Chairman of the Shubert Organization, on the set of Cats, *about 1986.*

Shubert would try to sell off its theatres. Schoenfeld and Jacobs, however, disclaimed the idea. The *New York Times* reported in 1972 that, "far from selling properties in the theatrical district, the Shubert interests were intensifying their efforts to improve the area. Increasing pressure is being put on the city to rid the area of prostitutes and stores and movie houses that deal in pornography." As Schoenfeld

Lee and J.J.'s Shubert Alley at the time of the seventy-fifth anniversary cele-
bration of the Booth Theatre, and their flagship house, the Sam S. Shubert.

would explain to McMorrow in 1977, he and Jacobs had approached
the problem "from several angles, investing millions in productions,
looking for plays that would develop new audiences, funding projects
like the half-price Time Square ticket booth, becoming active in
cleaning up the theatre district."

A little more than a decade later, the Broadway theatre is arguably in better shape as a result of their efforts. It depends on whom you talk to, of course. There is a continuing controversy which involves "the Shuberts"—as Schoenfeld and Jacobs are known—and other theatre owners, on the one hand, and those interested in landmarking Broadway theatres, several of which have been replaced by new buildings. A major lawsuit on the issue is in the offing. Certainly Times Square is changing. Most would say for the better, although there are those who argue that the theatre district is being robbed of its traditional character by the office towers that are rising everywhere along Broadway.

The Shuberts have been producing again for more than a decade, and presenting some immensely successful shows, among them *Ain't Misbehavin'* and *Dancin'* in 1978, *Amadeus* and *Children of a Lesser God* in 1980, *Dreamgirls* and *Nicholas Nickleby* in 1981, and more recently *Cats, Sunday in the Park with George,* and *Jerome Robbins' Broadway.* They own sixteen theatres on Broadway, and a half interest in another, and they own or operate five more theatres on the road. The consent decree signed in the fifties has recently been lifted, and the Shuberts are free to expand as they see fit. Whether it would be worthwhile for them to do so is unclear.

The road has never really come back in any significant way, and probably never will. Production costs are skyrocketing, and with them ticket prices, as well. The total number of shows opening on Broadway and the total number of theatre weeks played in any season are both declining. In any given week, a number of theatres stand empty. Musicals often do spectacularly well, but it becomes increasingly difficult to find a producer for a straight play on Broadway. It is argued that plays with serious content have become box office poison. But all of this is perhaps not very new; Broadway, as somebody once said, is *always* at a low ebb. Still, grosses are up, and the 1988–1989 season was the most profitable ever. All of the traditional ironies are still there.

As these last lines are being written, the seventy-fifth anniversary celebration of Lee and J.J.'s Shubert and Booth Theatres and Shubert

Alley has just taken place. The Alley remains a dramatic piece of open space in a neighborhood where space has been at a premium for more than three-quarters of a century. It looks airier and less romantic now than in the old photographs from Lee and J.J.'s day, but somehow the effect is still right. Shubert Alley remains the symbol of Broadway show business and a fitting memorial to the three extraordinary Shubert brothers.

SELECTED BIBLIOGRAPHY

As I have explained in the Preface, many of the sources used in the preparation of *The Shuberts of Broadway* are unpublished. Letters, press releases, reports, contracts, and other manuscript materials may be consulted in the Shubert Archive. Period newspaper and magazine articles about the Shuberts, as well as reviews of Shubert shows, may also be found there, in the files of the former Shubert press office. I have often quoted from books that contain insights into the activities and personalities of the Shuberts. In particular, I have drawn on works that the general reader might not otherwise be likely to encounter. The list below includes those works, as well as other sources that provided useful background for this book and that may be of interest to readers who would like to continue to explore the Broadway of Sam, Lee and J.J. Shubert.

Adams, Joey, *Here's to the Friars* (New York: Crown, 1976).

Adams, Samuel Hopkins, *A. Woollcott* (New York: Reynal and Hitchcock, 1945).

Allen, Fred, *Much Ado About Me* (Boston: Little, Brown, 1956).

Atkinson, Brooks, *Broadway* (New York: Macmillan, 1974).

Baral, Robert, *Revue* (New York: Fleet, 1962).

Belasco, David, *The Theatre Through the Stage Door,* edited by Louis V. DeFoe (New York: Harper, 1919).

Bernheim, Alfred L., *The Business of Theatre* (New York: Actors' Equity Association, 1932).

Best Plays series, various editors (New York: Dodd, Mead, 1916—.).

Binns, Archie, *Mrs. Fiske and the American Theatre* (New York: Crown, 1955).

Bishop, Jim, *The Mark Hellinger Story* (New York: Appleton-Century-Crofts, 1952).

Bordman, Gerald, *American Musical Comedy* (New York: Oxford University Press, 1982).

———, *American Musical Revue* (New York: Oxford University Press, 1985).

———, *American Musical Theatre* (New York: Oxford University Press, 1978).

———, *American Operetta* (New York: Oxford University Press, 1981).

———, *Jerome Kern* (New York: Oxford University Press, 1980).

Botto, Louis, *At This Theatre* (New York: Dodd, Mead, 1984).

Brady, William A. *Showman* (New York: E.P. Dutton, 1937).

Brockett, Oscar G., and Robert R. Findlay, *Century of Innovation* (Englewood Cliffs, N.J.: Prentice-Hall, 1973).

Brown, Jared, *The Fabulous Lunts* (New York: Atheneum, 1986).

Carter, Randolph, *The World of Flo Ziegfeld* (New York: Praeger, 1974).

Charters, Ann, *Nobody: The Story of Bert Williams* (New York: Macmillan, 1970).

Churchill, Allen, *The Great White Way* (New York: E.P. Dutton, 1962).

Clarke, Norman, *The Mighty Hippodrome* (New York: A.S. Barnes, 1968).

Coad, Oral S., and Edwin Mims, Jr., *The American Stage.* Vol. 14 of *The Pageant of America* (New Haven: Yale University Press, 1929).

Davis, Owen, *I'd Like To Do It Again* (New York: Farrar and Rinehart, 1931).

Engel, Lehman, *The American Musical Theatre* (New York: Macmillan, 1975).

Erenberg, Lewis A., *Steppin' Out* (Westport, Conn.: Greenwood Press, 1981).

Ewen, David, *The Book of European Light Opera* (New York: Holt, Rinehart and Winston, 1962).

Farnsworth, Marjorie, *The Ziegfeld Follies* (London: Peter Davies, 1956).

Ford, Corey, *The Time of Laughter* (Boston: Little, Brown, 1967).

Fowler, Gene, *Schnozzola* (New York: Viking, 1951).

Foy, Eddie, and Alvin F. Harlow, *Clowning Through Life* (New York: E.P. Dutton, 1928).

Freedman, Samuel G., "Shubert Archive Sorts Treasures of the Stage," *New York Times,* Sept. 25, 1985.

Frick, John W., and Carlton Ward, eds., *Directory of Historic American Theatres* (Westport, Conn.: Greenwood Press, 1987).

Frick, John W., *New York's First Theatrical Center* (Ann Arbor, Mich.: UMI Research Press, 1985).

Frohman, Daniel, *Daniel Frohman Presents* (New York: Claude Kendall and Willoughby Sharp, 1935).

Gaver, Jack, *Curtain Calls* (New York: Dodd, Mead, 1949).

Gilbert, Douglas, *American Vaudeville* (New York: Dover, 1963).

Golden, John, and Viola Brothers Shore, *Stage-Struck John Golden* (New York: Samuel French, 1930).

Goldman, Herbert G., *Jolson* (New York: Oxford University Press, 1988).

Goldstein, Malcolm, *George S. Kaufman* (New York: Oxford University Press, 1979).

Gordon, Max (with Lewis Funke), *Max Gordon Presents* (New York: Bernard Geis, 1963).

Gordon, Ruth, *My Side* (New York: Harper and Row, 1976).

Grau, Robert, *Forty Years Observation of Music and the Drama* (New York: Broadway Publishing Co., 1909).

Green, Abel, and Joe Laurie, Jr., *Show Biz from Vaude to Video* (New York: Henry Holt, 1951).

Green, Stanley, *Broadway Musicals* (Milwaukee: Hal Leonard Books, 1985).

———, *Broadway Musicals of the 30s* (New York: Da Capo, 1071).

———, *The World of Musical Comedy* (San Diego: A.S. Barnes, 1980).

Harding, Alfred, *The Revolt of the Actors* (New York: William Morrow, 1929).

Harris, Warren G., *The Other Marilyn* (New York: Arbor House, 1985).

Hayes, Helen (with Sanford Dody), *On Reflection* (London: W.H. Allen, 1969).

Henderson, Mary C., *The City and the Theatre* (Clifton, N.J.: James T. White, 1973).

———, *Theater in America* (New York: Abrams, 1986).

Hopkins, Arthur, *Reference Point* (New York: Samuel French, 1948).

Hopper, DeWolf, *Reminiscences of DeWolf Hopper* (Garden City, N.Y.: Garden City Publishing Co., 1927).

Hornblow, Arthur, *A History of the Theatre in America*, 2 vols. (Philadelphia: J.B. Lippincott, 1919).

Hughes, Glenn, *A History of the American Theatre, 1700–1950* (New York: Samuel French, 1951).

Isman, Felix, *Weber and Fields* (New York: Boni and Liveright, 1924).

Israel, Lee, *Miss Tallulah Bankhead* (New York: G.P. Putnam's Sons, 1972).

Jessel, George (with John Austin), *The World I Lived In* (Chicago: Henry Regnery, 1975).

Kislan, Richard, *Hoofing on Broadway* (New York: Prentice-Hall, 1987).

Knapp, Margaret, "A Historical Study of the Legitimate Playhouses on West Forty-second Street Between Seventh and Eighth Avenues in New York City" (Ph.D. diss., City University of New York, 1982).

Lahr, John, *Notes on a Cowardly Lion* (New York: Alfred A. Knopf, 1969).

Laufe, Abe, *The Wicked Stage* (New York: Frederick Ungar, 1978).

Leavitt, M.B., *Fifty Years in Theatrical Management* (New York: Broadway Publishing, 1912).

Leonard, William, ed., *Chicago Stagebill Yearbook, 1947* (Chicago: Chicago Stagebill, 1947).

Lewis, Kevin, "A World Across from Broadway: The Shuberts and the Movies," *Film History*, vol. 1, no. 1, 1987.

———, "A World Across from Broadway (II): Filmography of the World Film Corporation, 1913–1922," *Film History*, vol. 1, no. 2, 1987.

Liebling, A.J., "The Boys from Syracuse," *The New Yorker* (Nov. 18, 25, Dec. 2, 1939).

Lifson, David S., *The Yiddish Theatre in America* (New York: Thomas Yoseloff, 1965).

Mc Arthur, Benjamin, *Actors and American Culture, 1880–2910* (Philadelphia: Temple University Press, 1984).

Mc Cabe, John, *The Man Who Owned Broadway* (New York: Doubleday, 1973).

Marcosson, Isaac F., and Daniel Frohman, *Charles Frohman: Manager and Man* (New York: Harper and Brothers, 1916).

Mates, Julian, *America's Musical Stage: Two Hundred Years of Musical Theatre* (Westport, Conn.: Greenwood Press, 1985).

Morehouse, Ward, *George M. Cohan* (Philadelphia: J.B. Lippincott, 1943).

Morell, Parker, *Lillian Russell* (New York: Random House, 1940).

Morosco, Helen M., and Leonard Dugger, *Life of Oliver Morosco: The Oracle of Broadway* (Caldwell, Idaho: Caxton Printing, 1944).

Mosedale, John, *The Men Who Invented Broadway* (New York: Richard Marek, 1981).

Mulholland, Jim, *The Abbott and Costello Book* (New York: Popular Library, 1977).

"The Passing Show," newsletter, various editors (New York: The Shubert Archive, 1977—.).

Poggi, Jack, *Theater in America: The Impact of Economic Forces, 1870–1967* (Ithaca: Cornell University Press, 1968).

Powers, James T., *Twinkle Little Star* (New York: G.P. Putnam, 1939).

Quinn, Arthur Hobson, *A History of the American Drama from the Beginning to the Present Day*, 2 vols. (New York: Appleton-Century-Crofts, 1923–27).

Sexton, R.W., and B.F. Betts, eds., *American Theatres of Today* (New York: Architectural Book Publishing Co., 1927).

Sieben, Pearl, *The Immortal Jolson* (New York: Frederick Fell, 1962).

Skinner, Otis, *Footlights and Spotlights* (Indianapolis: Bobbs-Merrill, 1923).

Slide, Anthony, *The Vaudevillians* (Westport, Conn.: Arlington House, 1981).

Smith, Cecil, *Musical Comedy in America* (New York: Theater Arts Books, 1950).

Sobol, Louis, *The Longest Street* (New York: Crown, 1968).

Stagg, Jerry, *The Brothers Shubert* (New York: Random House, 1968).

Stoddart, Dayton, *Lord Broadway* (New York: Wilfred Funk, 1941).

Strang, Lewis C., *Celebrated Comedians of Light Opera and Musical Comedy in America* (Boston: L.C. Page, 1901).

Taubman, Howard, *The Making of the American Theatre* (New York: Coward, McCann and Geoghegan, 1965).

Timberlake, Craig, *The Life and Works of David Belasco, the Bishop of Broadway* (New York: Library Publishers, 1954).

Williams, Henry B., ed., *The American Theatre: A Sum of Its Parts* (New York: Samuel French, 1971).

Wilson, Francis, *Francis Wilson's Life of Himself* (Boston: Houghton Mifflin, 1924).

Wilson, Garff, *A History of American Acting* (Bloomington: Indiana University Press, 1966).

———, *Three Hundred Years of Drama and Theatre* (Englewood Cliffs, N.J.: Prentice-Hall, 1973).

Wilstach, Paul, *Richard Mansfield* (New York: Charles Scribner's Sons, 1908).

Winter, William, *Life and Art of Richard Mansfield*, 2 vols. (New York: Moffat, Yard, 1910).

———, *Life of David Belasco*, 2 vols. (New York: Moffat, Yard, 1918).

Wodehouse, P.G., and Guy Bolton, *Bring on the Girls* (New York: Simon and Schuster, 1953).

Young, William, ed., *Famous American Playhouses, 1716–1971*, 2 vols. (Chicago: American Library Association, 1973).

INDEX